BE MADE WHOLE: THE FIVE DIMENSIONS OF HEALING
WITH DAILY SELF-HELP PRACTICES

ERIC JOSEPH

COPYRIGHT © 2024 BY ERIC W. JOSEPH. ALL RIGHTS RESERVED.

No part of this book may be reproduced or used in any manner without written permission of the copyright owner except for the use of quotations in a book review. For more information, address: totaltherapytoday@gmail.com.

Unless otherwise indicated, all scriptures are taken from THE HOLY BIBLE, ENGLISH STANDARD VERSION (ESV): Scriptures taken from THE HOLY BIBLE, ENGLISH STANDARD VERSION ® Copyright© 2001 by Crossway, a publishing ministry of Good News Publishers and used by permission.

Scriptures marked NIV are taken from the NEW INTERNATIONAL VERSION (NIV): Scripture is taken from THE HOLY BIBLE, NEW INTERNATIONAL VERSION ®. Copyright© 1973, 1978, 1984, 2011 by Biblica, Inc.™. Used by permission of Zondervan

Book paperback edition: January 2024

Book design, Cover design, and eBook design by: mahabulmondol74@gmail.com

Publisher: Amazon KDP

ISBN 979-8-9877156-5-9 (Hardcover)

ISBN 979-8-9877156-4-2 (Paperback)

ISBN 979-8-9877156-3-5 (eBook)

Library of Congress Control Number: 2023924329

www.totaltherapytoday.com

DEDICATION PAGE

The book is a big, heartfelt shout-out to my incredible parents who have found their eternal home in Heaven– my mom, the legendary "J," and my dad, the one and only "Papa." Now, let me spill the tea on J – she's not just your average mom; she was the Christian veteran who steered me through the wild journey of growing up. Her prayers? They were like secret superpowers that turned me into this incredible human whose book you're reading.

And then there's Papa, the work ethic wizard with a side of dad jokes. Picture this: he was hard-working, joke-cracking, and wisdom-dropping like confetti. So, this book isn't just a bunch of words on paper; it's a giant virtual hug to J and Papa. Their love shaped me, their teachings guided me, and their laughter echoed in my life's soundtrack. No matter where life takes me, they've got a permanent spot in the VIP section of my heart. Here's to J, the prayer powerhouse, and Papa, the work master-— thanks for being the real MVPs in my personal and Christian life journey!

Table of Contents

INTRODUCTION

CHAPTER 1: THE JOURNEY TO WHOLENESS: EXAMINING THE FIVE DIMENSIONS OF HEALING

CHAPTER 2: SPIRITUAL HEALING: RESTORING THE CONNECTION WITH GOD

- Spiritual Wounds Caused Within the Church
- Healing from Spiritual Wounds
- Exploring the Role of Scripture, Prayer, and Faith in Spiritual Healing

CHAPTER 3: MENTAL HEALING: RENEWING THE MIND

- Methods for Developing a Positive Mindset

CHAPTER 4: EMOTIONAL HEALING: NAVIGATING AND PROCESSING OUR EMOTIONS

- Childhood Traumas
- Understanding Emotional Wounds

CHAPTER 5: RELATIONAL HEALING: RESTORING & BUILDING HEALTHY CONNECTIONS

- The Impact of Relational Wounds
- Exploring the Impact of Broken Relationships and the Importance of Healthy Connections

CHAPTER 6: PHYSICAL HEALING: NURTURING AND CARING FOR OUR BODIES

- The Impact of Chronic Stress and Worry on our Physical Health
- The Impact of Fasting on Our Physical Health

CHAPTER 7: INTEGRATING THE DIMENSIONS: HOW THE 5 DIMENSIONS SUPPORT EACH OTHER

CHAPTER 8: OVERCOMING CHALLENGES; ADDRESSING BARRIERS

CHAPTER 9: TOOLS AND PRACTICAL APPROACHES TO HEALING
Investigating the Origin of the Five-Dimensional Wounds
CHAPTER 10: LIVING A WHOLENESS-CENTERED LIFE
Integrating Wholeness: An Overview of the Main Ideas and Findings
CONCLUSION

PREFACE

Welcome to the transformative journey of "Be Made Whole: The 5 Dimensions of Healing." Within the pages of this book, we embark on a profound exploration of healing in its myriad forms, delving deep into the intricate tapestry of the human experience. Drawing inspiration from the timeless wisdom of the Bible, we uncover the divine gift of total healing that spans our spiritual, emotional, mental, relational, and physical well-being.

The scriptures serve as our guiding light, revealing chapters illuminating the various dimensions of healing. These sacred texts offer direction and encouragement and convey the divine intention to experience wholeness in every facet of our lives. Psalm 147:3 provides solace in the spiritual realm of healing, reassuring us that God "heals the brokenhearted and binds up their wounds." This verse underscores the interconnectedness of our spiritual and physical health. As we draw closer to God, we open ourselves to significant healing in our souls, fostering a holistic sense of well-being. Throughout this journey, we will navigate the rich tapestry of biblical wisdom, uncovering profound insights illuminating the path to complete healing across the various dimensions of our existence.

A profound scriptural reminder of God's ability to bring healing, joy, and restoration, even amidst our emotional pain, is found in Isaiah 61:3. This verse beautifully articulates God's promise to replace our despair with a "crown of beauty" in place of ashes and to anoint us with the "oil of joy" instead of mourning. It serves as a poignant expression of the emotional facets of the healing process. The foundation for mental healing is eloquently laid out in Romans 12:2, urging us to undergo a transformative journey by "the renewing of [our] mind." This verse underscores the decisive role of God's Word and the guidance of the Holy Spirit in breaking free from detrimental thought patterns. Through this process, we can experience a profound shift in our mental landscape, fostering clarity and peace that emanate from a renewed mind.

Colossians 3:13 highlights the importance of healing within relationships, urging us to "bear with each other and forgive one another if any of you has a grievance against someone." Cultivating humility, forgiveness, and a commitment to fostering love and understanding becomes crucial for restoring relationships, allowing God's healing grace to mend fractured bonds. Moreover, James 5:14–15 sheds light on the physical dimension of healing, emphasizing the role of faith-based prayer in restoring and maintaining bodily health. The Bible affirms God's concern for our physical well-being, encouraging us to seek His healing touch, whether through the expertise of medical professionals or supernatural intervention.

Let the Bible serve as our guiding light, illuminating the path to wholeness and healing in every aspect of our lives. As we approach its teachings with an open heart, we position ourselves to absorb the wisdom and discernment that can help us fully embrace God's healing love.

This book is a wellspring of motivation, support, and practical advice as we navigate the daily challenges in our quest for total healing. Let us embrace the transformative power of God's love, anticipating a future abundant with the richness of wholeness.

With heartfelt intentions for the well-being of humanity.

Eric Joseph

INTRODUCTION

THE EFFECTS OF SIN: EXPOSING THE BROKENNESS OF HUMANITY

Have you ever wondered why our world is infested by such pervasive misery, grief, and brokenness? The perplexing nature of why individuals inflict harm upon one another and, at times, succumb to making regrettable decisions can be disconcerting. Delving into the intricacies of this matter reveals that the repercussions of sin, actions that deviate from God's intended purpose for our lives, lie at the heart of the issue. This chapter explores the damaging effects of sin, shedding light on how it has left people broken and grappling with the consequences of their choices.

When Adam and Eve, the inaugural figures in human history, chose to defy God's guidance within the serene confines of the Garden of Eden, the profound consequences of their disobedience reverberated throughout the Earth. The enduring repercussions of their transgressions continue to resonate in our lives today. Each of us, including you and me, bears the weight of this legacy, having fallen short of God's impeccable standard. As articulated in Romans 3:23, "For all have sinned and fall short of the glory of God," the universal nature of this human condition is underscored.

The pervasive impact of sin is observable across various facets of our existence. Our connections with God, fellow humans, and even ourselves bear this fundamental flaw's undeniable imprint.

To comprehend the intricacies of these effects, let us delve into each realm of our lives impacted by the enduring consequences of sin.

Initially, sin introduces a profound division between humanity and its Creator, God. The conscious decision to engage in sinful behavior erects a formidable barrier that obstructs our ability to fully embrace the love and presence of God, as articulated in Isaiah 59:2: "But your iniquities have separated you from your God; your sins have hidden his face from you." This results in a palpable spiritual disconnection, creating a yearning for reconciliation with our heavenly Father.

The ramifications of our transgressions extend beyond mere separation; they render us incapable of fostering a personal and intimate relationship with God's immaculate and sacred nature. Sin erects an insurmountable wall that hinders our capacity to grasp and appreciate God's love, guidance, and benevolent gifts. Consequently, we find ourselves grappling with a sense of purposelessness, emptiness, and a profound sense of loss due to this estrangement. The destructive nature of sin dismantles the harmonious relationship God originally intended us to enjoy with Him.

Additionally, sin hurts how we connect with others. When we lie, deceive, or injure others, it creates problems in our relationships. In Galatians 5:19–21, the Bible talks about actions that harm connections, such as unfriendly, envious, angry, or selfish. These actions don't just affect us, but they also hurt those around us by causing conflicts and problems. Sin makes us selfish and unkind to others.

It leads us to prioritize our desires over the well-being of others. Feelings of envy, resentment, and jealousy take over and spoil our relationships. Instead of showing love and respect, we often end up causing harm and betraying each other. Sin can affect how we feel and think, and it can mess with our overall well-being—our emotions, thoughts, and even our physical health. When we go against what God says in the Bible, it often leads to some harsh consequences. As Proverbs 13:15 puts it, "Bad choices make life hard." This can leave us feeling empty, sad, and guilty.

Sin disrupted our emotions and thoughts, sending us down a not-so-great path. It can lead to habits that are hard to break, routines that hurt us, and decisions that end up being harmful. It steals away our happiness, joy, and that calm feeling inside. And the results of our sins, like regret, shame, and guilt, can weigh us down. Sin affects our well-being incorrectly, causing problems for our emotions, thoughts, and body. When we go against God's rules, we often face the not-so-nice consequences of our actions. As Proverbs 13:15 says, "Bad choices make life tough." This can lead to feelings of emptiness, sadness, and guilt. Sin messes up our feelings and thoughts, putting us on a harmful path. It can lead to habits like addiction, unhealthy routines, and choices that harm us. Sin takes away our happiness, joy, and inner peace. We end up dealing with the results of our mistakes, feeling sorry, embarrassed, and guilty.

CHAPTER 1: THE JOURNEY TO WHOLENESS: EXAMINING THE FIVE DIMENSIONS OF HEALING

In this opening chapter, we dive into the basic concept of healing in every way as we start a journey to become whole. We'll examine how healing works in our spirit, mind, emotions, relationships, and body. It's essential to grasp and care for each part because they all contribute to our health. This way, we can achieve lasting and significant healing.

- **Understanding Wholeness and Healing:** Let's explain what "wholeness" means and its importance. Wholeness goes beyond just not having physical illnesses or feeling emotionally upset. It's about being well and balanced in every part of our life. We'll talk about how healing involves a complete change that looks at our body, mind, and spirit together instead of just focusing on one part of our life.

- **Healing:** What Is It? Healing is a journey of profound renewal and revival. It's the beautiful way our body, mind, and spirit come back to life, like a broken bone getting better or a plant bouncing back after a trim. Healing is like giving a warm hug to every part of who we are, saying, "You're important, and I wish for you to be complete!" It's like a superpower that brings strength, energy, and wellness to all aspects of our being.

- **The Spiritual Dimension of Healing:** In this section, we delved into the spiritual side of healing. We discussed how feeling spiritually down and alone comes from the gap caused by sin between people and God. Using examples from the Bible, we will discuss the importance of building up our faith and reconnecting with God to fix this spiritual hurt. Next, we'll see how prayer, reading scripture, and other spiritual practices can strengthen our bond with God, leading to spiritual wholeness.

- **The Mental Dimension of Healing:** Our mental health dramatically impacts how we heal. Let's examine how mental obstacles, unhelpful ideas, and negative attitudes can slow our progress and well-being. We'll check out simple ways to refresh our thoughts, build positive thinking habits, and embrace a mindset of growth and resilience. We'll get inspiration from the Bible, psychology, and medical sources to make everything practical and easy to understand.

- **The Emotional Dimension of Healing:** Emotional wounds can impact our lives, making it more challenging to feel whole. Recognizing our sadness and pain as we explore our emotional well-being is essential. We'll discover ways to better handle and understand our emotions, using simple techniques for caring for ourselves, healing emotionally, and building our emotional strength. We'll tap into insights from psychology and the Bible to guide us in this journey.

- **The Relational Dimension of Healing:** Building strong connections with others is crucial for our happiness, but sometimes, things go wrong, and conflicts can strain our relationships. This book dives into how these challenges affect our healing journey. Using simple language, psychological ideas, and stories from the Bible, we'll learn how to handle conflicts, forgive, and build positive relationships. These skills will help us feel complete and supported in our lives.

- **The Physical Dimension of Healing:** A close relationship exists between physical health and general well-being. We'll explore the importance of taking good care of our bodies by eating right, exercising, and practicing self-care. Based on scripture and scientific and medical studies, we will also discover the significant influence of a healthy lifestyle on our physical well-being and how it helps us on our path to wholeness.

- **The Connection Between the Dimensions:** Instead of being separate pieces, the five healing dimensions are intertwined threads that make up our entire self. They come together like a puzzle, creating a beautiful picture of wholeness. When we care for and nurture each part, a balanced harmony is formed, leading to overall well-being.

CONCLUSION: In this section, we've laid the foundation for our journey toward wholeness by exploring the five dimensions of healing. We've acknowledged how our spiritual, mental, emotional, relational, and physical aspects depend on each other. With an understanding of the significance of each dimension and its impact on our overall health, we're ready to start a transformative journey toward recovery and completeness.

In the upcoming sections, we'll delve deeper into each dimension, exploring practical methods, biblical insights, and scientific findings to guide us in achieving complete healing. Together, we'll discover how to lead a life of wholeness, restoration, and abundance through the power of faith, self-reflection, meaningful relationships, and self-care practices.

CHAPTER 2: SPIRITUAL HEALING: RESTORING THE CONNECTION WITH GOD

Spiritual healing aims to revive and strengthen your spiritual well-being and connection with God. This transformative process focuses on healing emotional and psychological wounds and addressing past experiences, beliefs, or relationships with the spiritual realm.

In spiritual healing, we explore the essential journey of reconnecting with God, our Creator. Let's examine the five spiritual wounds that originated from the transgression of Adam and Eve and understand how Jesus serves as the source of spiritual healing.

- **The Spiritual Wounds Caused by Sin:** When Adam and Eve chose not to follow God's will, sin entered the world. This created a gap between God and us, like a spiritual distance. Because of this separation, we started having strong desires, making us feel disconnected from our heavenly Father.

- **Guilt and Shame:** When Adam and Eve realized they had done wrong, they felt terrible and ashamed. Similarly, we all carry the weight of feeling embarrassed about our mistakes. These feelings create a barrier between us and God, making it hard to feel spiritually complete truly.

Sins make it challenging to see how much God loves us and is always with us. It's like a fog that makes it tricky to understand what God wants for us and why we're here. Sin keeps us stuck in harmful thoughts and actions. Things like being too focused on ourselves and other bad habits keep us from growing spiritually and getting closer to God.

- **Spiritual Blindness:** Spiritual blindness happens when we make mistakes and lose our connection with God's always-there, life-giving presence. Without spiritual well-being, we miss out on the deep relationship with God that we were meant to enjoy.

Jesus Christ is the one who can fix our spiritual wounds. He does this by making up for our mistakes through His death and returning to life. He allows us spiritually healed and renewed by bringing people closer to God with His love, kindness, and mercy. John 3:16 says, "God loved the world so much that He gave His only Son. Anyone who believes in Him will not be lost but will have eternal life." You can also find this idea in 2 Corinthians 5:17-18: "So if someone belongs to Christ, they become a new person. The old things are gone; now everything is new! All this is from God, who brought us back to Himself through Christ."

- **Spiritual Healing Through Jesus Christ:** The Holy Spirit does a beautiful work within us, bringing a refreshing renewal to our hearts and minds, molding us to mirror the likeness of Christ. Through this spiritual rebirth, we receive forgiveness for our sins and are empowered to lead lives that align with God's divine plan. The Scriptures inspire us with these words: "Do not conform to the pattern of this world but be transformed by the renewing of your mind. Then you can test and approve God's will—his good, pleasing, and perfect will." - Romans 12:2, 3.

- **Freedom from Bondage:** We find freedom from the shackles of sin through Jesus. Our spiritual well-being plays a crucial role in this liberation. Jesus' victory over sin and death empowers us to break free from the restraints that once held us captive. This newfound freedom allows us to live spiritually liberated lives, surrendering to God's will. As it is written, "Who the Son sets you free, you are truly free." - John 8, verse 36.

Spiritual Wounds Caused Within the Church

While church leaders are meant to be a source of encouragement, guidance, and spiritual support, there are moments when their actions or attitudes may, knowingly or unknowingly, cause spiritual harm to members. Spiritual wounds are deep emotional or psychological hurts related to one's faith, beliefs, or spiritual journey. These wounds stem from interactions or relationships that challenge, deceive, or disturb a person's connection with God, sense of spirituality, or acceptance within a religious community.

Such injuries can also arise from interactions with fellow churchgoers or personal struggles with faith.

Spiritual wounds manifest as emotional pain, diminished trust in others, or challenges in forming solid spiritual connections. They can lead to disconnection, doubt, or confusion about one's beliefs. Here are ten signs of spiritual wounds that a Christian may need to address for healing:

- **Spiritual Abuse:** Spiritual abuse is a distressing phenomenon within religious communities, where individuals in positions of spiritual authority exploit their power in harmful ways. At its core, spiritual abuse involves the misuse of religious influence to manipulate and control believers, often leaving them emotionally scarred. This mistreatment can manifest in various forms, such as coercive tactics, manipulation of scripture, and the imposition of rigid doctrinal beliefs.

One general aspect of spiritual abuse is the exertion of control over church members. Leaders may exploit their positions to dictate members' lives beyond the spiritual realm, including personal choices, relationships, and even career decisions. This control extends to enforcing strict adherence to particular doctrines, stifling dissent, or questioning established beliefs.

The emotional impact of spiritual abuse is profound, as victims often grapple with feelings of fear, guilt, and shame. The perpetrators may use spiritual teachings to instill a sense of unworthiness or to create a climate of constant judgment, making individuals question their worthiness in the eyes of God. This emotional manipulation can result in long-lasting psychological trauma, affecting not only an individual's spiritual well-being but also their overall mental health.

Furthermore, spiritual abuse can lead to a distorted understanding of faith and spirituality. Individuals subjected to such mistreatment may develop a skewed perception of God, associating the divine with judgment and condemnation rather than love and grace. This distortion can hinder their spiritual growth and prevent them from experiencing the transformative power of a healthy and nurturing spiritual community.

Addressing spiritual abuse requires creating awareness within religious communities, fostering open dialogue about healthy spiritual practices, and empowering individuals to recognize and report abuse. By promoting an environment of love, compassion, and understanding rooted in Christian principles, communities can work towards healing and preventing the detrimental effects of spiritual abuse on faithful followers seeking solace and guidance within their religious institutions.

- **Emotional manipulation:** Spiritual abuse extends beyond the misuse of spiritual authority and often involves dynamic manipulation tactics. Emotional manipulation refers to using strategies that exploit the emotions of churchgoers, aiming to influence their beliefs and behaviors. This insidious practice includes techniques like guilt-tripping, where individuals are made to feel responsible for imagined wrongs, and humiliation, where their dignity is undermined to maintain control.

Furthermore, spiritual abusers may exploit the vulnerabilities of church members, taking advantage of their weaknesses or insecurities.

This could involve manipulating individuals during moments of emotional fragility, coercing them into certain beliefs or actions. The perpetrators may create an atmosphere of fear, making it difficult for churchgoers to question or resist their authority.

In combating spiritual abuse, it becomes crucial to recognize the signs of emotional manipulation and empower church communities to foster environments of trust, openness, and support. By promoting emotional well-being and educating on healthy spiritual leadership, societies can guard against the detrimental effects of emotional manipulation within the sacred context of their faith.

- **Excessive Legalism**: Sometimes, people in the church can get too caught up in making lots of strict rules, like telling you exactly what to wear, what jewelry to have, or what food to eat. This kind of strictness is called excessive legalism. It's like putting a heavy load of rules on everyone, making it hard to focus on the gospel's central message and grow spiritually personally. Instead of feeling free and joyful in your faith, you might feel restricted and weighed down by all these detailed regulations. It's essential to strike a balance, understanding that faith is more than just following a long list of rules. Embracing the core message of love, compassion, and spiritual growth helps maintain a healthy and liberating religious experience without unnecessary burdens that hinder personal connection with God.

- **Hypocrisy:** Spiritual hypocrisy emerges when leaders in the church demonstrate a stark contrast between their actions and professed beliefs, leading churchgoers to feel disillusioned and lose trust. It resembles the familiar saying, "Do as I say, but not as I do." This contradiction between preached values and actual behavior creates a sense of betrayal among the faithful, eroding the foundation of trust within the church community.

Leaders failing to embody their teaching principles undermines the church's moral authority. Churchgoers who look to these leaders for guidance and inspiration can experience confusion and disappointment. The gap between words and deeds becomes a stumbling block to spiritual growth. Consequently, individuals may question the authenticity of the teachings and the sincerity of those imparting them.

Addressing spiritual hypocrisy is crucial for maintaining a healthy and vibrant church community. Leaders must strive to align their actions with their professed beliefs, fostering an environment where churchgoers can trust in the authenticity of the spiritual guidance they receive. This alignment not only preserves the integrity of the faith community but also nurtures the spiritual well-being of its members.

- **Neglect or Indifference**: Neglect or indifference in a church setting can be deeply hurtful. It happens when members seeking guidance or assistance need to receive the pastoral care and, support they require. This lack of attention can make them feel overlooked, unimportant, or abandoned.

In a faith community, where people often turn for solace and understanding, neglect can create a sense of isolation and disconnect.

Imagine reaching out for spiritual guidance and finding no one to lend an empathetic ear or offer comforting words.

This form of spiritual neglect can have lasting effects, eroding the congregation's sense of belonging and trust. Church leaders and fellow members must be mindful of each other's needs, providing the necessary care and support. Acts of kindness, compassion, and attentive listening can go a long way in fostering a sense of community and ensuring that no one feels left behind on their spiritual journey. In a loving and supportive church environment, everyone should feel valued and embraced, reinforcing the teachings of love and compassion central to the Christian faith.

- **Lack of Transparency:** In a church setting, transparency can harm the congregation's growth and well-being. When leaders fail to communicate openly and honestly, it creates an atmosphere of secrecy, concealing internal disagreements or issues. This lack of transparency fosters confusion and prevents the church members from fully understanding the dynamics.

By withholding crucial information, leaders inadvertently create an environment where rumors and misunderstandings thrive. These uncertainties hinder the spiritual development of the churchgoers, as they may grapple with unanswered questions and unaddressed concerns.

Open communication is essential for fostering trust and unity within a spiritual community. When leaders prioritize transparency, they empower the congregation to navigate challenges with clarity and confidence in the collective journey of faith. In essence, embracing openness contributes to a healthier spiritual environment where individuals can grow in their faith without the hindrance of unnecessary barriers.

- **Judgmental Attitude**: A critical attitude is like wearing glasses that only see mistakes and shortcomings. It's when someone focuses on pointing out faults instead of embracing acceptance, love, and understanding. Imagine a friend who always magnifies your slip-ups and flaws, making you feel small and criticized. This critical stance can be harmful, creating an atmosphere of negativity and fear. In a Christian context, it goes against compassion, forgiveness, and acceptance teachings.

In a loving Christian community, the emphasis should be on understanding and helping one another grow spiritually. On the contrary, a judgmental attitude can lead to feelings of inadequacy and shame, hindering the development of a supportive and nurturing environment. It's important to remember that everyone has imperfections, and a compassionate approach that recognizes these imperfections while offering love and support is more aligned with Christian principles. By fostering an atmosphere of acceptance, Christians can create a space where individuals feel valued and encouraged on their spiritual journey.

- **Spiritual Manipulation for Personal Gain**: This involves exploiting religious beliefs to fulfill personal desires and taking advantage of people's faith and trust to gain material, financial, or emotional benefits. In this deceptive practice, some spiritual leaders maintain control by claiming such things as "God told me to tell you" or insisting that specific actions or contributions are divinely mandated.

These manipulative tactics play on the vulnerability of individuals who trust in their spiritual leaders. The perpetrators may misuse sacred connections, asserting divine authority to justify their requests or demands. This creates a power dynamic where followers feel compelled to comply, fearing consequences if they resist. The manipulation often extends to emotional and psychological levels, instilling a sense of obligation and dependency on the manipulator.

This form of spiritual exploitation not only harms individuals on a personal level but also tarnishes the integrity of the spiritual community. Believers must be discerning and vigilant, recognizing genuine spiritual guidance from manipulative tactics that serve personal interests rather than the community's well-being.

- **Exclusion or Rejection**: These behaviors create tension and division within the Christian community by singling out and sidelining specific individuals or groups due to factors like their background, beliefs, or way of life. This kind of exclusion fosters feelings of rejection and alienation among those affected.

Such actions go against the inclusive nature of Christian teachings, which emphasize love and acceptance for all. Instead of embracing diversity, exclusion, and rejection contradict the core principles of Christianity, causing emotional harm and undermining the sense of belonging within the body of Christ. In essence, this form of spiritual abuse deviates from the Christian message of unity and compassion, perpetuating a climate of discord and hurt. Addressing these issues is vital for restoring a healthy, inclusive environment where Christian values of love, understanding, and acceptance flourish, promoting a genuine sense of community among believers.

- **Unresolved Conflict Handling**: Spiritual abuse within a church extends beyond mishandling disputes; it involves the creation of a toxic environment and failing to promote healing, forgiveness, and reconciliation. In some instances, church leaders may exploit their positions, manipulating power dynamics to control and harm church members emotionally. This can create an atmosphere filled with fear, guilt, and shame.

While many church leaders earnestly serve and uplift their congregations, it's crucial to acknowledge that not all adhere to these positive practices. When wounds from spiritual abuse emerge, individuals should seek guidance from trustworthy spiritual mentors, counselors, or other professionals within the Christian community. These supportive figures can help navigate the complexities of healing, forgiveness, and reconciliation.

Emphasizing these values in the aftermath of spiritual abuse is vital for fostering a healthier and more nurturing environment within the church community, where individuals can find solace and renewal in their faith.

Healing from Spiritual Wounds

Navigating the path of healing from spiritual wounds within the church context is intricate and delicate. This journey often addresses feelings of letdown, betrayal, or disillusionment stemming from religious encounters or interactions with fellow church members and leaders.

Acknowledging and affirming the pain caused by spiritual wounds is crucial to discovering solace in God's embrace and attaining emotional release. The Bible advocates for genuine expression of emotions in the presence of God, as emphasized in Psalm 34:18 (ESV): "The Lord is near to the brokenhearted and saves the crushed in spirit." This scripture underscores the divine closeness and deliverance available to those grappling with emotional distress.

- **Seek Out a Supportive Community**: Spiritual Abuse involves misusing authority to manipulate church members, leading to fear, guilt, or shame. The Bible encourages communal strength, emphasizing the benefits of unity in Ecclesiastes 4:9–10. The verse illustrates the value of companionship, stating, "Two are better than one because they have a good reward for their toil." In times of difficulty, having a supportive community is crucial, echoing the sentiment, "If one falls, the other will help them up." Seek solace and understanding within a caring church family or support group to share struggles and receive compassion and assistance.

- **Spend time in The Word:** Spiritual abuse is the misuse of authority to control believers, causing emotional pain. It's crucial to remember Psalm 119:105, which says, "Your word is a lamp to my feet and a light to my path." This verse emphasizes the guiding power of God's Word, offering comfort and direction. In times of spiritual healing, turning to scripture provides solace and insight. By grounding oneself in the teachings of the Bible, individuals can find strength and clarity, allowing the light of God's wisdom to illuminate their journey. Seek guidance in His Word, a trustworthy beacon in navigating life's complexities.

- **Pray for Healing and Guidance**: Spiritual abuse involves the misuse of spiritual authority within the church, manipulating believers and causing emotional distress. In the Christian faith, Philippians 4:6-7 encourages believers to bring their concerns to God through prayer, thanking Him. This practice invites God's peace and guidance into the healing journey. The ease of God, surpassing human understanding, becomes a shield for the hearts and minds of those in Christ Jesus.

It emphasizes the importance of relying on God's wisdom and comfort amid challenges, reinforcing a spiritual approach to overcoming the negative impact of spiritual abuse within the church community.

- **Learn to Lean & Practice Forgiveness**: In Christianity, forgiveness holds a central role, echoing the words of Colossians 3:13 (ESV): "Bearing with one another and, if one has a complaint against another, forgiving each other; as the Lord has forgiven you, so you also must forgive." However, spiritual abuse, marked by the misuse of authority to manipulate and instill fear, guilt, or shame, poses a challenge to this divine principle. Such misuse disrupts the healing power of forgiveness, hindering the congregation's ability to embody the Lord's mercy. Overcoming spiritual abuse involves acknowledging the hurt, seeking support, and applying biblical forgiveness principles to restore harmony within the church.

- **Reflect on Your Spiritual Self:** Psalm 139:23–24 (ESV) invites believers to let God examine their hearts: "Search me, O God, and know my heart! Try me and find out what I think! And see if there be any grievous way in me, and lead me in the way everlasting." This psalm encourages a sincere prayer for self-awareness and divine guidance. God's humble request is to explore our innermost thoughts, identify wrong paths, and guide us eternally and righteously. It emphasizes a deep connection with God, acknowledging our need for His insight and direction in our spiritual journey.

- **Find Renewal through Service and Worship**: Engaging in worship and acts of service promotes spiritual renewal and a connection to God and others. Hebrews 10:24–25 (ESV) calls for communal worship, saying, "And let us consider how to stir up one another to love and good works, not neglecting to meet together, as is the habit of some, but encouraging one another, and all the more as you see the Day drawing near."

- **Consider Getting Professional Help**: Proverbs 12:15 (ESV) says, "The way of a fool is right in his own eyes, but a wise man listens to advice." Getting professional help aligns with the biblical value of seeking wise counsel. A trained counselor or spiritual mentor can provide insightful advice and support during healing.

Drawing from scripture and seeking guidance from supportive sources can provide strength and hope as you navigate the path of healing and spiritual growth. It is crucial to keep in mind that healing from spiritual wounds is a process that involves seeking support, spiritual reflection, prayer, forgiveness, and finding renewal in your faith.

Exploring the Role of Scripture, Prayer, and Faith in Spiritual Healing

Scripture, prayer, and faith are powerful tools that can transform our lives, bringing us closer to feeling spiritually whole. Imagine faith as a strong belief in God's love and power to heal. It's about trusting that God is reliable, offering forgiveness and healing. Hebrews 11:6 says, "Without faith, it's impossible to please him." This means to get close to God, we must believe in His existence and that He rewards those who seek Him.

Faith also means letting go of control and relying on God's guidance. Trust God's plan; Proverbs 3:5–6 says, "Trust in the Lord with all your heart and do not depend on your understanding. Acknowledge Him, and He will show you which path to take."

We ask God for wisdom and guidance through prayer, inviting Him to lead us on the healing path. We share our burdens with Him and seek His direction in our lives. James 1:5 says, "If any of you lacks wisdom, let him ask God, who gives generously to all without reproach, and it will be given him."

Prayer also brings comfort and peace in times of distress and brokenness. It allows us to find refuge in God's presence, knowing He is our source of comfort and strength. According to Philippians 4:6-7, "Do not be anxious about anything, but in everything by prayer and supplication with thanksgiving let your requests be made known to God. And the peace of God, which surpasses all understanding, will guard your hearts and minds in Christ Jesus."

The Bible, God's special message to us, is like a guidebook filled with advice, wisdom, and good promises for our spiritual well-being. When we read the Bible, it helps us understand God's thoughts, and it shows us what is true. The Bible's words can change our thoughts, steering us from negative thoughts and guiding us toward God's healing promises. Romans 12:2 tells us, "Don't copy the behavior and customs of this world but let God transform you into a new person by changing how you think. Then you will learn to know God's will for you, which is good, pleasing, and perfect."

The Bible also reminds us about God's faithfulness, love for us, and the assurance that He is always with us. It gives us hope and comfort as we seek healing in our spiritual journey. Romans 15:4 says, "Such things were written in the Scriptures long ago to teach us. And the Scriptures give us hope and encouragement as we wait patiently for God's promises to be fulfilled."

To start your journey toward spiritual healing, you can begin by setting aside time for prayer and thinking deeply about God's teachings. Ask God for guidance and wisdom, and read the Bible regularly.

Make these practices a crucial part of your daily routine. Today, you can purposefully strengthen your faith, deepen your connection with God through prayer, and engage more with the teachings in the Bible.

- **A Prayer for Spiritual Healing**: Merciful and Loving God, I come before You with a humble heart, asking for Your healing touch on my wounded spirit. This is a prayer for spiritual healing, where I bring my uncertainties, worries, and brokenness to the cross. I accept Jesus Christ as my Lord and Savior and turn away from my sins, seeking Your mercy. Please, let Your Spirit flow into me, giving me the strength to avoid wrongdoing. May Your love and peace fill my heart, dispelling my darkness. Bring healing and a deep sense of spiritual comfort and ease. With Jesus as my guide, I now hold onto hope, grace, and forgiveness. Thank You for salvation and spiritual healing in Jesus' name, Amen!

CHAPTER 3: MENTAL HEALING: RENEWING THE MIND

Transformation happens when our minds are made new. Taking care of our mental well-being is crucial because harm to our senses can hinder our growth, inner peace, and overall joy. Thankfully, through the strength of Jesus Christ, we can experience healing and renewal, leading to lasting change. Below, we'll explore the five common mental challenges, their connection to Adam and Eve's actions, and how seeking healing from Jesus can make a significant difference.

Mental wounds are any hurts or traumas that impact a person's emotions and thinking abilities. These wounds can weigh us down and affect our daily lives. It's like carrying a heavy burden that makes it difficult to experience the fullness of life. With answers, here are five common mental wounds:

- **Post-Traumatic Stress Condition (PTSD):** After going through a challenging and scary situation, some folks might experience something called PTSD. It's like a heavy anxiety feeling that sticks around after a significant trauma, like a bad accident, a fight, or something frightening. Trauma can happen from just one event or a bunch of them, like a nasty fight, a natural disaster, or a violent situation. When someone has PTSD, they might have flashbacks and bad dreams, keep thinking about the scary stuff, try to avoid reminders of it, be super alert all the time, and even feel emotionally numb. This can make it hard for them to do everyday things and enjoy life like they used to.

- **Major Depressive illness (MDD):** Known as Depression, Major Depressive Disorder (MDD) is a mood sickness characterized by long-lasting sadness and hopelessness, along with a lack of interest or joy in most activities. People with MDD may also have trouble concentrating, feelings of not being valuable, persistent thoughts of death or suicide, and changes in sleep, eating, and energy patterns.

Various factors, including imbalances in brain chemicals, life events, and a genetic tendency, can trigger depression.

- **Anxiety Disorders:** In life, we face various challenges related to worry and fear, which are like different kinds of troubles. These troubles can be compared to anxiety disorders, such as feeling overwhelmed by panic, being anxious in social situations, having constant worry, or being very scared of specific things. These challenges can make it hard for us to go about our daily lives and follow God's path.

When we struggle with these worries, our bodies may react in different ways, like sweating, shaking, a fast heartbeat, or problems with our stomach. These physical signs can be like warning signals that something is not correct.

The causes and symptoms of these worries can vary, depending on our challenge.

Remember, just as Jesus offered comfort and guidance to those in distress, seeking support from friends, family, and our faith community can help us navigate these challenges. Let's trust in God's love and seek help when needed.

- **Borderline Personality Disorder (BPD):** This is a challenging condition that affects a person's relationships, emotions, and how they see themselves. People with this condition may feel intense loneliness and fear and engage in activities that harm themselves. They might also act impulsively and struggle to control their emotions, experiencing constant emptiness. It is a condition where individuals face inner turmoil and may need support and understanding.

- **Substance Use Disorders (SUD):** Despite the negative impact it brings, the persistent use of drugs or alcohol is a crucial aspect of substance use disorders. These issues can significantly damage a person's social connections, career prospects, and well-being. Individuals dealing with substance use disorders may find themselves both physically and mentally reliant on the substance, leading to withdrawal symptoms when attempting to quit.

It is crucial to recognize that various psychological, environmental, and hereditary factors often combine to create intricate and multifaceted mental challenges.

Seeking help from mental health professionals, such as therapists, counselors, or psychiatrists, is essential for addressing and recovering from these issues, as they can differ from person to person.

- **Anxiety and dread**: Worry and fear that stick around for a long time are often linked to stress, a common mental struggle. This ongoing concern and discomfort is rooted in the peace and calm that existed before sin came into the world. In the beginning, Adam and Eve lived in perfect harmony and stability in the Garden of Eden alongside God and nature. However, uneasiness and insecurity became part of the human experience after they disobeyed.

Medical and psychiatric experts explain that various things can cause anxiety disorders and fear-based reactions. Past experiences, stresses from the environment, and imbalances in brain chemicals are some factors that can bring about these feelings of worry and fear. Understanding these aspects is crucial in dealing with anxiety and finding ways to overcome it.

In the biblical account from Genesis 3:8–10, it's narrated that the man and his wife sensed the presence of the Lord God as He moved through the garden in the cool evening breeze. Filled with a sense of fear, they sought refuge among the trees. When the Lord God addressed the man, he admitted, "I heard you walking in the garden, so I hid. I was afraid because I was naked."

This passage is part of the story of Adam and Eve's disobedience in the Garden of Eden. It captures the moment they become aware of their nakedness and attempt to conceal themselves from the divine presence. The vivid imagery, such as the Lord God moving in the garden and the calm evening winds, adds depth to the narrative. The man's admission of fear and shame further highlights the consequences of their disobedience. This biblical account is a powerful metaphor for the human experience of guilt, shame, and the instinct to hide when confronted with wrongdoing.

- **Depression:** Depression, a widespread mental struggle, is marked by persistent feelings of sadness, disinterest, and a profound sense of emptiness. It mirrors the rupture of Adam and Eve's once-perfect connection with God and the world, disrupted by the destructive impact of sin. The weight of sin has left an enduring effect, giving rise to symptoms of depression in individuals. As articulated in Psalm 42:5, the question echoes, "Why am I so discouraged? Why is my heart so sad?" Yet, amidst the despair, a ray of hope is expressed in the resolve to thank God, the ultimate source of salvation. This biblical reflection encapsulates the complexity of the emotional struggle, acknowledging the impact of brokenness while hinting at the possibility of redemption. Understanding depression as a multifaceted battle allows for empathy and compassion, recognizing the need for support and gratitude as steps toward healing and restoration.

- **Low Self-Esteem:** Low self-esteem is like a wound in your mind, making you see yourself in a not-so-great way. It's when you feel not good enough and worthless. The story of Adam and Eve in the Bible shows how this messed-up feeling has been around for a long time. When they did something wrong, they suddenly felt embarrassed and tried to hide from God.

The book of Genesis says they even stitched together some leaves to cover up. They heard God coming, and instead of being cool about it, they got scared and hid among the trees.

This story is like a snapshot of how low self-esteem can make you act. You might want to hide and not feel good enough, just like Adam and Eve did. But the good news is that talking about these feelings and getting help can be like getting rid of those fig leaves – finding a way to be more open and less covered up.

Trauma is a deep psychological wound caused by overwhelming and distressing events that we struggle to cope with. While it's not directly linked to Adam and Eve's sin, the brokenness it introduced to the world has led to tragic events throughout history. These distressing incidents can seriously impact our mental well-being, leading to conditions like post-traumatic stress disorder (PTSD) and other trauma-related issues.

Addiction, on the other hand, is a psychological injury marked by an unhealthy and obsessive dependence on drugs, alcohol, or other activities. The initial harmony in human desires was disrupted by the brokenness caused by sin. Consequently, individuals may turn to addictive substances or behaviors, attempting to fill the void left by the absence of a close connection with God and the resulting shattered emotional state. Both trauma and addiction highlight the profound impact of brokenness on our mental health, necessitating understanding, support, and professional help for healing and recovery. I've realized a deep truth about life: I often do the opposite even when I sincerely aim to do what's right (Romans 7:21–25, NLT). My heart holds a genuine love for God's law, yet my thoughts wrestle with an opposing force within me. It's like I'm bound to this sinful nature, a slave to the wrong things.

It's disheartening—I feel like such a mess, trapped in a life fueled by sin and leading toward death. Who can rescue me from this predicament? Thankfully, the answer lies in Jesus Christ, our Lord. He's the game-changer, the solution to my struggle. Though I genuinely want to align my thoughts with God's rules, I find myself trapped by the pull of sin due to my flawed nature. It's a paradox that only Christ can untangle, offering redemption and freedom from the clutches of a life driven by corruption.

Understanding the impact of brokenness on our mental health begins with recognizing the roots of mental scars in the story of Adam and Eve. Despite this, there is a pathway to recovery and healing through Jesus Christ's life, death, and resurrection. Placing our trust in Him brings a peace that goes beyond understanding (Philippians 4:7) and casts away fear with His pure love (1 John 4:18). Jesus invites us to discover our identity and value in Him (Ephesians 2:10), offering solace, hope, and mental healing in acknowledgment of our suffering.

In addition to spiritual healing, seeking professional assistance like therapy or counseling becomes crucial for addressing and healing mental traumas. Combining therapeutic approaches with biblical principles can serve as valuable tools to comprehend and treat mental health issues. Integrating both spiritual and professional dimensions creates a holistic approach that recognizes the complexity of mental well-being and the diverse ways individuals find healing and restoration.

Ultimately, the sin of Adam and Eve is identified as the primary cause of mental wounds, disrupting our sense of safety and calmness. Common mental injuries like addiction, trauma, depression, anxiety, and low self-esteem stem from this sin. However, there's hope for recovery, peace, and healing through Jesus Christ. Embracing His love, seeking professional help, and incorporating biblical principles into our lives initiate the journey of mental healing, leading to the fulfillment intended by God.

In today's society, mental health issues are prevalent, and prolonged stress can significantly impact the occurrence and severity of these conditions. While stress is a normal response to challenging or dangerous situations, its persistence and excessiveness can severely negatively affect mental health. Let's explore the connection between chronic stress and anxiety disorders, depression, and other mental health issues.

As previously explained, anxiety disorders involve overwhelming and persistent feelings of worry, fear, and unease. Chronic stress, continually triggering the body's stress response and elevating vigilance levels, can lead to may contribute to the development of anxiety disorders.

The continuous release of stress hormones such as cortisol can disrupt the balance of neurotransmitters in the brain, impairing mood regulation and worsening anxiety symptoms. In Philippians 4:6-7, the Bible advises, "Do not be anxious about anything, but in every situation, by prayer and petition, with thanksgiving, present your requests to God. And the peace of God, which transcends all understanding, will guard your hearts and minds in Christ Jesus," offering guidance for managing anxiety.

Similarly, depression is a mood disorder characterized by a lack of motivation, persistent feelings of sadness, and diminished interest or pleasure. Chronic stress can exacerbate depression by exceeding the body's capacity to handle stress and reducing serotonin levels in the brain, which are crucial for mood regulation. Prolonged activation of the stress response may lead to despair, hopelessness, and a decreased ability to experience joy.

Those dealing with depression find comfort in Psalm 34:17–18, which states, "The LORD is close to the brokenhearted and saves those who are crushed in spirit. The righteous cry out, and the LORD hears them; he delivers them from all their troubles."

Other mental health challenges, such as obsessive-compulsive disorder (OCD), drug use disorders, and post-traumatic stress disorder (PTSD), can emerge or intensify due to prolonged stress. Traumatic events, ongoing pressures, or a mix of both can significantly impact the brain's stress response system, making a person more prone to various illnesses. A comforting scripture in Isaiah 41:10 reminds those facing tough times: "So do not fear, for I am with you; do not be dismayed, for I am your God.

I will strengthen, help, and uphold you with my righteous right hand."

The connection between mental health issues and chronic stress involves complex interactions among biological, psychological, and environmental factors. Stress has the potential to change the brain's structure and function, disrupt neurotransmitter systems, and affect inflammation and the immune system, contributing to the onset or exacerbation of mental health disorders.

When persistent stress negatively impacts mental health, seeking support becomes crucial. Treatment approaches may include a combination of counseling, therapy, medication, and self-care techniques. Consulting with mental health specialists can provide valuable insights, coping strategies, and personalized treatments tailored to individual needs.

Several self-care techniques, in addition to expert assistance, can aid in the management of ongoing stress and advance mental health:

- **Stress management strategies:** You may lower stress levels and foster calm by practicing progressive muscle relaxation, mindfulness meditation, or deep breathing.

SOCIAL SUPPORT:

- Establishing contact with loved ones.

- Attending support groups.

- Seeking professional help can offer a secure area to communicate thoughts, concerns, and emotional support.

GOOD LIVING PRACTICES:

- Taking part in regular exercise.

- Keeping a balanced diet.

- Resilience and general mental health can be enhanced by getting adequate sleep.

CREATING LIMITS:

- The ability to refuse.
- Making self-care a priority.
- Setting appropriate limits can help manage stress and avoid overload.

- **Seeking Expert Advice:** It's critical to get in touch with mental health specialists for advice, evaluation, and treatment choices if long-term stress and its detrimental effects on mental health become too much to handle. Understanding the link between long-term stress and mental illnesses and getting the right help can help people's mental health. It's critical to remember that each person's path is different and that developing successful stress management and mental health promotion techniques may call for perseverance, patience, and a comprehensive approach.

Methods for Developing a Positive Mindset

Our thoughts wield significant influence over our beliefs, emotions, and behaviors. To cultivate better mental health and bolster resilience, it's crucial to acquire practical techniques for reframing negative thoughts and fostering a positive mental outlook. Let's explore practical methods for overcoming negative thought patterns and cultivating optimism.

- **Spotting Cognitive Distortions**: Cognitive distortions are negative thinking processes that can skew our perception of the world. Recognizing common distortions such as overgeneralization, personalizing, and all-or-nothing thinking is the initial step in addressing and rephrasing negative thought patterns. Achieving awareness is pivotal for confronting and transforming these mental patterns. (Source: David D. Burns, "Feeling Good: The New Mood Therapy")

- **Journaling and Thought Records:** Maintaining a journal is a powerful tool for examining and identifying negative thinking patterns. Putting our thoughts on paper lets us discern recurring negative themes and scrutinize their underlying assumptions. Thought records, a specific journaling technique, aid in confronting and reframing negative beliefs. (Source: "Cognitive Therapy Techniques: A Practitioner's Guide" - Leahy, Robert L.)

- **Practicing Gratitude:** Gratitude is a transformative discipline that redirects our focus from what we lack to what we have. Regularly expressing thanks for life's blessings, irrespective of size, contributes to developing a positive outlook. Engaging in practices such as writing thank-you cards, maintaining a gratitude journal, and reflecting on happy moments proves effective in cultivating gratitude. (Source: Robert A. Emmons, "Gratitude Works: A 21-Day Program for Creating Emotional Prosperity")

- **Positive Self-Talk and Affirmations:** Affirmations, positive declarations that counteract negative self-talk, play a vital role in altering the way we speak to ourselves. Deliberately repeating affirmations aligned with our goals and positive attributes fosters optimism, bolsters self-esteem, and nurtures self-compassion. (Source: Matthew McKay et al., "Self-Esteem: A Proven Program of Cognitive Techniques for Assessing, Improving, and Maintaining Your Self-Esteem")

- **Cognitive Restructuring Techniques:** Cognitive restructuring involves identifying negative thoughts, evaluating their validity, and replacing them with more rational and constructive thoughts. We can effectively change negative thought patterns by scrutinizing facts, challenging irrational ideas, and considering alternative perspectives. (Source: "Mind Over Mood: Change How You Feel by Changing the Way You Think" - Dennis Greenberger and colleagues)

- **Perspective Shifting and Reframing:** Reframing entails approaching a problem differently and developing a new perception. Actively seeking optimistic or growth-oriented viewpoints allows challenges to be viewed as learning and personal development opportunities. Reframing enables us to redirect our attention from negativity to a more positive perspective. (Source: Karen Reivich et al., "The Resilience Factor: 7 Keys to Finding Your Inner Strength and Overcoming Life's Hurdles")

Cultivating a positive mindset and breaking free from negative thought habits demands awareness, effort, and persistence. By integrating these methods into our daily routines, we can progressively reshape our thought processes and witness the profound impact of maintaining a positive outlook. Remember, you can mold your thoughts into something more fulfilling. Take intentional steps to overcome negativity and embrace the strength of positive thinking.

- **A Prayer for Mental Healing**: Dear Heavenly Father, I approach You in moments of sorrow, seeking Your grace to heal my mind. I acknowledge the burdens, worries, and mental challenges I carry. I pray for peace and mental recovery. Please grant me the clarity to release the weight on my mind and the courage to face my mental obstacles.

Please guide me in seeking assistance when needed.

Calm, love, and soothe my mind, directing me to maintain cheerful and upbeat thoughts. I trust in Your ability to bring healing to my mind and provide an unexplained calmness. In the gracious and loving name of Jesus, Amen.

CHAPTER 4: EMOTIONAL HEALING: NAVIGATING AND PROCESSING OUR EMOTIONS

This chapter delves into the significant impact of emotional wounds and emphasizes the crucial aspect of emotional healing. Emotions are a vital part of our human experience, but the effects of sin have led to various emotional wounds that can negatively affect our well-being. These wounds are psychological injuries resulting from multiple backgrounds and life events, influencing how a person perceives and navigates the world. Let's explore five common emotional wounds that individuals may encounter throughout their lives.

1. **Rejection and Abandonment**: Experiencing rejection and abandonment can leave profound emotional scars. These wounds often originate from being rejected or abandoned by caregivers, romantic partners, friends, or social groups. Such experiences may lead to feelings of unworthiness, fear of intimacy, and challenges in forming trusting relationships.
2. **Betrayal:** Betrayal involves a breach of trust and confidence in someone or something we believe in. This emotional wound can arise from various situations, such as infidelity in a relationship, a friend betraying confidence, or a business partner acting dishonestly. Betrayal can result in anger, hurt, and a reluctance to trust others in the future.
3. **Grief and Loss**: Grief and loss are natural responses to losing someone or something significant, such as the death of a loved one, the end of a relationship, or the loss of a job. Coping with grief can be emotionally challenging and may lead to feelings of sadness, loneliness, and emptiness.
4. **Humiliation and Shame**: Experiences of embarrassment and shame can harm one's self-esteem and self-worth. These wounds often stem from situations where individuals feel publicly embarrassed, judged, or criticized. People may internalize these

feelings, grappling with a persistent sense of inadequacy or unworthiness.
5. **Injustice and Trauma**: Encountering injustice or trauma can result in lasting emotional wounds. Traumatic events, including experiences such as accidents, physical or sexual abuse, or witnessing violence., can lead to post-traumatic stress, anxiety, and feelings of powerlessness.

Additionally, emotional wounds may manifest in various ways, including:

- Persistent Sadness: Emotional wounds often manifest as enduring sadness or emptiness that doesn't seem to fade over time.
- Anxiety and Fear: Emotional wounds can contribute to increased anxiety and fear, leading to excessive worrying, phobias, or panic attacks.
- Low Self-Esteem: Damaged self-esteem is another sign of emotional wounds, causing feelings of inadequacy and self-doubt.

- Difficulty Trusting Others: Individuals with emotional wounds may struggle to trust others, expecting betrayal and impacting their relationships.
- Recurring Flashbacks: Emotional trauma can result in recurring flashbacks to the traumatic event, causing distress and disruption.
- Social Isolation: Many people with emotional wounds tend to isolate themselves from others, withdrawing from social activities to protect themselves from further emotional pain.
- Physical Symptoms: Emotional wounds can also manifest physically, with symptoms such as chronic headaches, digestive issues, and autoimmune conditions linked to unaddressed emotional trauma.

Understanding and addressing these emotional wounds are crucial for comprehensive healing and well-being. Seeking support from mental health professionals can play a vital role in the journey toward emotional recovery.

Childhood Traumas

Childhood traumas have the potential to significantly influence an individual's life during adolescence and adulthood, often manifesting in behaviors and attitudes that may not be immediately apparent. Understanding the profound impact of early experiences is crucial for comprehending our actions, perceptions, and overall lifestyle. Here are examples to reflect upon:

1. **Physical Abuse**:

Childhood trauma frequently involves physical abuse, encompassing instances of enduring physical violence or harsh discipline. The aftermath of such abuse leaves both emotional and physical scars, affecting self-esteem, trust, and overall well-being.

2. **Emotional Abuse:**

Another prevalent form of childhood trauma is emotional abuse, characterized by constant criticism, humiliation, or manipulation by caregivers or authority figures. The enduring effects can lead to deep emotional wounds, impacting a person's psyche in the long term.

3. **Sexual Abuse:**

Childhood sexual abuse is a profoundly distressing form of trauma, resulting in survivors grappling with feelings of shame, guilt, and various emotional difficulties. Offering unwavering support and understanding is crucial for survivors navigating their healing journey.

4. **Neglect:**

Childhood neglect arises when caregivers fail to meet a child's basic needs, whether it be for food, shelter, or emotional support. This neglect can leave lasting emotional scars, giving rise to issues such as attachment difficulties and challenges related to self-worth.

5. **Witnessing violence**:

They are growing up in an environment where one witness domestic violence or community-related violence can be highly traumatic. Children exposed to such situations often experience anxiety, fear, and emotional instability.

6. **Loss or Abandonment**:

The loss of a parent, whether through death or abandonment, can inflict a profound emotional wound. Children may grapple with feelings of grief, rejection, and insecurity.

7. **Bullying:**

Childhood trauma can also result from bullying, occurring either in school or online. Emotional scars from bullying can persist into adulthood, affecting self-esteem, relationships, and mental health.

Recognizing that these emotional wounds can be interconnected, impacting various facets of a person's life is crucial. Healing from such wounds often necessitates self-awareness, support from loved ones, and, in some cases, professional counseling or therapy.

Understanding the origins of our emotional responses is the first step toward fostering a healthier and more resilient future.

Understanding Emotional Wounds

Rejection is a profound emotional wound rooted in the brokenness of sin, causing significant pain and distress. The feeling of being unloved, unwanted, or not belonging impacts our well-being, influencing thoughts, behaviors, and relationships. Originating from the disobedience of Adam and Eve in the Garden of Eden, their expulsion symbolizes the initial experience of rejection, separating them from God's intimate presence.

The story of Adam and Eve is a powerful illustration of the enduring effects of rejection throughout human history. The brokenness caused by sin perpetuates feelings of rejection in various forms—within relationships, communities, and oneself. The emotional scars of feeling unloved or unwanted linger, as highlighted in Genesis 3:23-24 (NLT), which recounts their banishment from Eden.

However, the narrative of rejection doesn't conclude with despair. God, in His boundless love and grace, addresses our brokenness through Jesus Christ. His sacrificial death and resurrection offer healing and restoration for emotional wounds. Despite experiencing rejection in His earthly ministry, Jesus extends acceptance and unconditional love to those who turn to Him.

Through faith in Jesus, solace and healing for wounded hearts are attainable, as emphasized in "Healing the Shame that Binds You" by John Bradshaw.

Understanding the psychological impact of rejection and its resulting wounds is crucial for the healing process. Therapy, counseling, and professional support equip individuals with tools to address and heal emotional wounds caused by rejection. Acknowledging these wounds is an essential step toward healing—recognizing the pain, validating emotions, and seeking support from God and others. Surrendering hurts to God invites His transformative acceptance and love into our lives.

Betrayal intensifies emotional pain when someone we trust violates that trust, as exemplified by the serpent deceiving Adam and Eve in the Garden of Eden (Genesis 3:13, NLT). Grief and loss, stemming from sin's brokenness, manifest in losing relationships, loved ones, or dreams. Genesis 3:16-19 details the consequences faced by Adam and Eve, emphasizing the profound grief and loss resulting from sin.

"The Grief Recovery Handbook: The Action Program for Moving Beyond Death, Divorce, and Other Losses" by James, John W. et al. serves as a source, underlining the importance of acknowledging and addressing grief and loss. Recognizing these emotional wounds is a pivotal step toward healing, involving validating pain, seeking support, and inviting God's healing presence into our lives.

- **Shame:** Deep-seated feelings of worthlessness and inadequacy often result from the awareness of our sin and the consequent brokenness. The immediate response of shame by Adam and Eve,

following their disobedience to God, is vividly portrayed in Genesis 3:7-8. Their attempt to cover themselves with fig leaves underscores the destructive nature of shame. The source of this insight is drawn from "Healing the Shame that Binds You" by John Bradshaw.
- **Fear and Anxiety:** Emotional wounds can harm our well-being, hindering our ability to live fully. The fear experienced by Adam and Eve after sinning, hiding from God, and anticipating punishment reflects the pervasive nature of fear in the human experience (Genesis 3:10, NLT). This perspective is enriched by "The Anxiety and Phobia Workbook" by Edmund J. Bourne.

The great news is that Jesus, through His sacrifice on the cross, offers forgiveness for our sins and the emotional healing accompanying it. Accepting and extending His forgiveness to ourselves and others allows us to experience emotional healing, as emphasized in 1 Peter 2:24.

God's unconditional love is a powerful source of healing our emotional wounds, providing comfort, security, and a sense of belonging (1 John 4:16, NLT). Being part of a supportive and loving community is instrumental in our emotional healing journey. Galatians 6:2 encourages us to share each other's burdens, fostering an environment where emotional processing and healing can occur. The exploration of emotional wounds, their origins in the sin of Adam and Eve, and the pathway to emotional recovery through Jesus provides a foundation for a journey of emotional restoration. Understanding common emotional wounds and embracing the healing power of Jesus allows us to experience the abundant life God intends for us.

Remember, you are not alone in your emotional struggles. Reach out to God, seek support from others, and embrace the healing power that God offers. Allow His love and grace to mend your emotional wounds, leading you to a place of wholeness and emotional well-being.

Understanding the Importance of Emotional Well-being in Overall Healing: Emotions play a crucial role in our mental, relational, physical, and spiritual well-being. Recognizing the significance of emotional well-being enables us to prioritize and cultivate a healthy, vibrant life, which is essential for holistic healing.

- **Emotions and Physical Health:** Scientific research underscores the vital link between emotions and physical health. Negative emotions, such as stress, anxiety, and anger, can manifest as physical symptoms, contributing to various health issues. Conversely, positive emotions like joy, gratitude, and contentment improve physical well-being ("Emotions and Health: The Overlooked Connection" by Robert Anderson).
- **Resilience:** Emotional well-being cultivates strength and the capacity to rebound from adversity. Developing emotional stability equips us with coping mechanisms to navigate life's challenges more effectively. It empowers us to face difficult circumstances positively and find healing amid adversity. It is referenced from "The Resilience Factor: 7 Keys to Finding Your Inner Strength and Overcoming Life's Hurdles" by Reivich, Karen, and Shatte, Andrew.

Recognizing that unaddressed emotional wounds can impede our overall healing is crucial. Past traumas, unresolved grief, and buried emotions can affect our well-being and hinder true wholeness. Acknowledging and addressing these emotional wounds is pivotal for our healing journey, as emphasized in "The Body Keeps the Score: Brain, Mind, and Body in the Healing of Trauma" by Van der Kolk, Bessel.

- **Emotional Intelligence:** Developing emotional intelligence enables adequate understanding and management of emotions. It encompasses self-awareness, self-regulation, empathy, and healthy interpersonal relationships. Cultivating emotional intelligence allows us to constructively navigate feelings and foster beneficial connections with ourselves and others. Insights from "Emotional Intelligence: Why It Can Matter More Than IQ" by Goleman, Daniel.

Our emotional well-being is intricately connected to our spiritual life. Aligning our emotions with spiritual values such as love, compassion, forgiveness, and gratitude enhances emotional well-being and brings us closer to spiritual wholeness. Colossians 3:12-14 (NLT) guides us: "Clothe yourselves with tenderhearted mercy, kindness, humility, gentleness, and patience. Accept each other's faults, and forgive anyone who offends you.

Remember, the Lord forgave you, so you must forgive others. Above all, clothe yourselves with love, which binds us all together in perfect harmony."

We acknowledge that releasing and surrendering emotional burdens to God is vital for healing. Offering our pain, hurt, and negative emotions to God opens us to His healing, bringing a sense of liberation and peace. Psalm 5:2 (NLT) reinforces this: "Listen to my cry for help, my King and my God, for I pray to no one but you."

Our emotional well-being is pivotal in our healing journey, influencing mental, relational, physical, and spiritual health. By recognizing the mind-body connection, addressing emotional wounds, developing emotional intelligence, and integrating our emotions with spiritual values, we can experience incredible healing and wholeness.

Action Steps for Managing and Healing Emotional Wounds and Traumas

This chapter delved into various action steps and techniques for effectively managing and healing emotional wounds and traumas. Emotional injuries can profoundly impact our well-being, but we can embark on a journey of healing and restoration with the right tools and support. By implementing these steps, we can navigate our emotional pain and find hope, resilience, and healing.

Self-Care Practices: Engaging in self-care activities, such as exercise, healthy eating, adequate rest, and relaxation techniques, nurtures our emotional well-being. These practices provide a foundation for self-care that supports our healing process, inspired by "The Self-Care Solution: A Modern Mother's Must-Have Guide to Health and Well-Being" by Mills, Julie.

- **Emotional Regulation Techniques:** Learning effective emotional regulation techniques, like deep breathing, mindfulness meditation, journaling, and grounding exercises, helps us manage intense emotions healthily. These techniques enable us to regain emotional balance and create space for healing, drawing from "The Dialectical Behavior Therapy Skills Workbook: Practical DBT Exercises for

- Learning Mindfulness, Interpersonal Effectiveness, Emotion Regulation, and Distress Tolerance" by McKay, Matthew et al.
- **Talk Therapy:** Individual counseling or psychotherapy provides a safe and supportive space to explore and process emotional wounds and traumas. Therapists use various approaches, including cognitive-behavioral therapy (CBT), psychodynamic therapy, and trauma-focused therapy, to facilitate healing and growth, as outlined in "Cognitive Behavioral Therapy: Basics and Beyond" by Beck, Judith.

Eye Movement Desensitization and Reprocessing (EMDR): EMDR is a therapeutic approach meticulously crafted to facilitate the processing and healing of traumatic memories. It ingeniously incorporates eye movements or other forms of bilateral stimulation to guide individuals through reprocessing traumatic experiences, thereby diminishing their emotional impact. Source: "Getting Past Your Past: Take Control of Your Life with Self-Help Techniques from EMDR Therapy" - Shapiro, Francine.

- **Support Groups:** Engaging in support groups, whether in person or online, can cultivate a profound sense of community and empathy. Being part of a collective of individuals who have weathered similar emotional wounds and traumas provides validation, shared experiences, and reciprocal support. Source: "The PTSD Workbook: Simple, Effective Techniques for Overcoming Traumatic Stress Symptoms" - Williams, Mary Beth.
- **Trusted Relationships:** Cultivating meaningful connections with family, friends, or spiritual mentors can be a cornerstone for emotional support and secure space for processing and healing. Sharing our emotions with trusted confidants offers comfort, empathy, and encouragement throughout the healing journey. Source: "The Gifts of Imperfection: Let Go of Who You Think You're Supposed to Be and Embrace Who You Are" - Brown, Brené.

In conclusion, effectively managing and healing emotional wounds and traumas necessitates a comprehensive approach encompassing self-care, emotional regulation, therapeutic interventions, and supportive relationships. By implementing these strategies, we embark on a path of healing, resilience, and personal growth. Remember that recovery is gradual, and practicing patience and self-compassion is indispensable. Embracing these strategies empowers us to navigate our emotional wounds and traumas with strength, emerging on the other side with enhanced emotional well-being and a rekindled sense of hope.

- **A Prayer for Emotional Healing:** Gracious Heavenly Father, I humbly seek Your divine touch for emotional healing in this vulnerable moment. I acknowledge the emotional wounds and turmoil I carry, the weight on my heart. I pray for Your comforting presence to mend the broken pieces of my emotions and calm the storms within. Grant me the strength to face my feelings, release what I've been holding onto, and find healing through Your boundless love.

Fill me with Your peace, joy, and resilience as I journey toward emotional restoration. Help me forgive, let go, and experience the fullness of Your grace in my vibrant life. In the compassionate and healing name of Jesus, I pray. Amen.

CHAPTER 5: RELATIONAL HEALING; RESTORING & BUILDING HEALTHY CONNECTIONS

Embarking on our journey toward wholeness, we delve into the profound significance of relational healing and explore practical strategies for restoring connections and cultivating robust relationships. Relationships, integral to our lives, mold our sense of belonging, love, and support. However, the impact of relational wounds on our well-being cannot be understated. We can undergo a transformative relational healing process by comprehending the origins of these wounds, seeking healing through a connection with Jesus, and implementing practical strategies.

Relational wounds encompass emotional injuries within interpersonal connections, influencing how individuals forge connections, trust, and communicate with others. These wounds have substantial and enduring effects on a person's well-being and capacity to establish healthy relationships. Here, we identify five prevalent forms of relational wounds:

1. **Betrayal of Trust:**

Betrayal unfolds when someone we trust breaches that trust through dishonesty, unfaithfulness, or divulging confidential information. This betrayal can evoke profound feelings of hurt and anger, diminishing our ability to trust in subsequent relationships. Its impact extends beyond friendships into the realm of romantic connections.

2. **Rejection and Abandonment:**

Experiencing rejection or abandonment, whether in childhood or adulthood, can be emotionally shattering. The aftermath of rejection often includes feelings of unworthiness and inadequacy, posing challenges in forming secure and healthy attachments with others. Fear of abandonment may further complicate emotional intimacy.

3. **Unresolved Conflict:**

Persistent and unresolved conflict within a relationship creates wounds that erode trust and emotional connection. Ineffective communication, ongoing arguments, and lingering issues foster emotional distance and dissatisfaction in the relationship.

4. Emotional Abuse:

Emotional abuse encompasses manipulative, controlling, or belittling behaviors that inflict significant emotional harm. This insidious form of abuse can leave victims feeling trapped, powerless, and emotionally scarred, exerting a detrimental impact on their overall well-being.

5. Lack of Emotional Intimacy:

Emotional intimacy involves cultivating a connection and vulnerability with a partner or friend. When emotional intimacy is lacking, individuals may experience a sense of emotional disconnection, unfulfillment, and loneliness within their relationships.

By acknowledging these common relational wounds and actively engaging in the healing process, individuals can create a renewed sense of connection, trust, and fulfillment in their relationships.

Recognizing the significance of healing from relational wounds underscores the importance of cultivating self-awareness, fostering open communication, and, when necessary, seeking professional support from counselors or therapists. The process of building and sustaining healthy relationships encompasses several key elements:

1. Acknowledging and Addressing Wounds:

It is crucial to understand and actively address any wounds within the relationship. This involves a commitment to self-reflection and a willingness to confront and work through past hurts.

2. Fostering Trust:

Trust is the foundation of any healthy relationship. Building and maintaining trust requires consistent honesty, reliability, and communication. Discussing concerns and expectations can contribute to developing a solid and trusting bond.

3. Creating a Supportive and Emotionally Safe Environment:

Establishing an environment that promotes personal growth and emotional safety is fundamental. This involves cultivating a space where individuals feel comfortable expressing themselves, sharing vulnerabilities, and experiencing personal development without fear of judgment.

In conclusion, the journey to healing and cultivating healthy relationships necessitates a combination of self-awareness, open communication, and, when needed, professional guidance. Individuals can pave the way for meaningful connections and personal growth within their relationships by actively addressing wounds, fostering trust, and creating a supportive environment.

The Impact of Relational Wounds

- **Betrayal and Broken Trust:** The wounds caused by betrayal and broken trust run deep, fostering feelings of hurt and anger and eroding the foundation of faith in relationships. Whether arising from dishonesty, infidelity, or unfulfilled promises, these wounds inflict substantial emotional pain and strain on the fabric of relationships. (Source: "Beyond Betrayal: Taking Charge of Your Life after Boyhood Sexual Abuse" - Carnes, Richard G.)
- **Rejection and Abandonment:** The enduring impact of rejection or abandonment leaves scars on our relational well-being, emanating from experiences in childhood, fractured friendships, or failed romantic relationships. The pain from such incidents can hinder our capacity to trust and form healthy connections with others. (Source: "The Journey from Abandonment to Healing: Turn the End of a Relationship into the Beginning of a New Life" - Anderson, Susan.)

The story of Adam and Eve in the Garden of Eden is a crucial narrative that sheds light on the origins of relational brokenness. Initially, God created Adam and Eve in His image, establishing a perfect, harmonious relationship with each other and Him. However, their disobedience to God's commandments introduced sin and shattered the ideal state.

When Adam and Eve succumbed to the temptation of the forbidden tree, they prioritized their desires over trusting in God's perfect plan. This act severed their intimate connection with God, resulting in feelings of shame, guilt, and separation. The rebellion not only fractured their relationship with God but also led to blame, shame, and a loss of trust between them. This original sin had profound consequences for humanity, manifesting as conflict, distrust, and broken relationships throughout history.

Yet, the story of Adam and Eve doesn't culminate in despair. God, in His boundless love and mercy, didn't abandon humanity to the brokenness caused by sin.

He devised a plan for restoration and redemption. Through Jesus Christ, God offered a path for reconciliation and healing in our relationships. Jesus, the Son of God, bore the weight of our sins on the cross, providing forgiveness, redemption, and the prospect of restored relationships through His victorious resurrection.

By placing our faith in Jesus, we can experience the transformative power of His love and grace. Surrendering our brokenness hurts, and relational wounds to Him initiates a process of healing and restoration. Embracing Jesus's teachings and following His example allows us to learn how to love, forgive, and cultivate healthy, God-honoring relationships. Jesus calls us to extend grace, show kindness, and practice forgiveness, reflecting His forgiveness and love, as expressed in Romans 5:12- 21 (NLT): "When Adam sinned, sin entered the world. Adam's sin brought death, so death spread to everyone, for everyone sinned."

Individuals transgressed even before the law was given, yet their actions were not imputed as sin since there was no law to violate. Nevertheless, all faced mortality—from the era of Adam to the period of Moses—even those who did not defy a specific divine command, as Adam did. Adam serves as a symbol, a prefiguration of Christ, who was yet to come. However, a crucial disparity exists between Adam's transgression and God's benevolent bestowal. Through the sin of this solitary man, Adam, death befell many.

Yet, even more extraordinary is God's surpassing grace and the gift of absolution bestowed upon many through the agency of Jesus Christ.

The outcome of God's gracious gift differs from the consequence of one man's transgression. Adam's sin led to condemnation, but God's assistance resulted in our reconciliation with God, notwithstanding our culpability for numerous crimes. Through the sin of Adam, death held sway over many. However, God's extraordinary grace and the gift of righteousness prevail, offering triumph over evil and death to all who receive it through Jesus Christ.

Indeed, Adam's transgression brings condemnation to all, but Christ's singular act of righteousness establishes a harmonious relationship with God and imparts new life to everyone. Through one person's disobedience, many became sinners, yet through another's obedience, many will be deemed righteous. God's law was given to illuminate the extent of humanity's sinfulness.

However, as transgressions multiplied, so did God's exceptional grace. In contrast to sin's dominion leading to death, God's unparalleled grace now reigns, bestowing us a righteous standing with God and culminating in eternal life through Jesus Christ our Lord.

In addition to the biblical teachings, psychological and counseling resources offer valuable insights into the repercussions of sin and brokenness on relationships. Diverse therapeutic methodologies underscore the significance of forgiveness, communication, and empathy in the restoration of fractured relationships and the cultivation of wholesome connections with others (Source: "The Forgiving Self: The Road from Resentment to Connection" - Worthington, Everett L.).

The transgression of Adam and Eve introduced relational discord into the world. However, through Jesus Christ, we can encounter restoration and healing within our relationships. By actively seeking forgiveness, extending grace, and emulating the example set by Jesus, we embark on a journey of relational healing, mending the ties that sin has severed.

Exploring the Impact of Broken Relationships and the Importance of Healthy Connections

Relationships are crucial in shaping our lives, influencing our experiences, and impacting our overall well-being. The profound effects of broken relationships are evident in emotional distress, mental strain, and even physical health problems. This chapter explores the repercussions of fractured connections and emphasizes cultivating healthy relationships, drawing insights from biblical, medical, and psychological perspectives.

- **Emotional Distress:** Broken relationships often result in profound emotional distress, giving rise to feelings of sadness, anger, and betrayal. The Bible recognizes and addresses the pain caused by such ruptures, stressing the imperative to heal and restore bonds (Psalm 147:3, Matthew 5:23-24). In line with this, psychological research underscores the impact of broken relationships on emotional well-being, emphasizing the importance of seeking healing. As Psalm 147:3(NLT) puts it, "He heals the brokenhearted and bandages their wounds," and Matthew 5:23-24(NLT) urges reconciliation before offering sacrifices, aligning with insights from the Holmes-Rahe Stress Inventory.

- **Mental Strain:** The toll of broken relationships extends to mental well-being, contributing to anxiety, depression, and other mental health challenges. The Bible highlights the significance of healthy relationships, cautioning against divisive behaviors (Proverbs 17:17(NLT), Ephesians 4:31-32(NLT)). Proverbs 17:17(NLT) states, "A friend is always loyal, and a brother is born to help in time of need." Ephesians 4:31-32(NLT) advises against negative emotions, urging kindness, tenderheartedness, and forgiveness, mirroring the holistic approach recommended by medical and psychological perspectives.
- **Physical Health Consequences:** The effects of broken relationships extend beyond emotional and mental well-being to impact physical health. The Bible acknowledges the interconnectedness of mind, body, and relationships, urging believers to pursue peace and unity (1 Corinthians 6:19-20(NLT), Colossians 3:13-14(NLT)). 1 Corinthians 6:19-20(NLT) reminds believers that their bodies are temples of the Holy Spirit and encourages honoring God with their bodies. Colossians 3:13-14(NLT) stresses allowing for each other's faults and forgiving offenses, echoing findings from medical research, such as those from the Mayo Clinic, that link chronic relationship distress to physical health issues.

Cultivating healthy connections and meaningful relationships is integral to emotional well-being. The Bible promotes love, compassion, and forgiveness in relationships (1 Corinthians 13:4-7(NLT), Ephesians 4:2-3(NLT)). 1 Corinthians 13:4-7(NLT) beautifully describes love's characteristics, emphasizing patience, kindness, humility, and forgiveness. Ephesians 4:2-3(NLT) advises humility, gentleness, and patience, highlighting the importance of unity and peace. Such a biblical approach fosters happiness, joy, and contentment. In alignment with positive psychology principles, psychological research underscores the vital role of social support and belongingness in promoting emotional resilience and overall well-being.

Healthy connections positively impact mental health, contributing to a sense of security, enhanced self-esteem, and overall psychological well-being. The Bible underscores the profound influence of positive relationships on mental wellness. Proverbs 27:9 (NLT) says, "The heartfelt counsel of a friend is as sweet as perfume and incense." Additionally, Philippians 2:3-4 (NLT) advocates for selflessness, urging individuals not to be selfish but to humbly consider others' interests, reinforcing the value of positive interpersonal connections.

In line with biblical principles, empirical evidence, such as the Harvard Study of Adult Development, supports the enduring benefits of healthy relationships for mental health and life satisfaction—referencing the Harvard Study of Adult Development.

Cultivating healthy connections is crucial for emotional and mental well-being and yields tangible physical health advantages. The Bible accentuates the significance of community and support in promoting holistic health. Galatians 6:2 (NLT) encourages sharing burdens, aligning with James 5:16 (NLT), which advocates confessing sins and praying for one another for healing. Medical research, including studies by the National Institute on Aging, substantiates that robust social support systems contribute to improved overall health, decreased rates of chronic diseases, and faster recovery from illnesses—citing the National Institute on Aging as a source.

The undeniable impact of broken relationships on emotional, mental, and physical well-being underscores the importance of healthy connections.

However, the power of nurturing relationships, drawing from biblical principles, medical research, and psychological studies, cannot be overstated. These sources consistently convey the significance of healthy relationships in fostering healing, well-being, and wholeness. By acknowledging the repercussions of broken relationships and prioritizing the cultivation of healthy connections, individuals can embark on a transformative journey of healing, restoration, and meaningful connections in their lives.

- **A Prayer for Relationship Healing**: Heavenly Father, I approach You humbly, seeking Your guidance and grace for relational healing. I acknowledge the brokenness and conflicts in my relationships, the pain, and the distance that strained my bonds with those I care about. Please grant me the wisdom to navigate these challenges, the strength to mend what has been torn, and the courage to seek forgiveness and reconciliation. Soften our hearts, foster understanding, and enable us to empathize with one another's perspectives. May our communication be infused with love, patience, and compassion as we work together to heal our wounds. Let Your love and peace flow through our relationships, bringing harmony, restoration, and the strength to build lasting connections. I offer this prayer in the name of Jesus, the ultimate source of love and unity. Amen.

CHAPTER 6: PHYSICAL HEALING: NURTURING AND CARING FOR OUR BODIES

This chapter emphasizes the importance of physical healing, the link between sin and its impact on our bodies, and the hope and restoration Jesus offers. We'll explore the five most common physical wounds, sicknesses, or diseases, their roots in the original sin of Adam and Eve, and how physical healing can be achieved through faith, medical care, and a holistic approach to well-being. Drawing insights from biblical, medical, and psychological sources will help us better understand the significance of physical healing and the path toward wholeness.

The story of Adam and Eve's disobedience in the Garden of Eden introduced sin into the world, resulting in brokenness and suffering, including physical ailments. The fall of humanity disrupted the perfect harmony between body, mind, and spirit, leading to various physical challenges, as stated in Genesis 3:16-19 NLT. Romans 8:20-22 (NLT) adds that all creation, against its will, was subjected to God's curse. However, with hopeful anticipation, the design looks forward to joining God's children in glorious freedom from death and decay. The passage mentions that all creation has been groaning in the pains of childbirth up to the present time.

From genetic disorders to lifestyle-related ailments, the brokenness caused by sin has impacted our physical well-being throughout generations. Psalm 38:3-11 (NLT) recognizes the connection between sin and physical suffering, stating, "Because of your anger, my whole body is sick; my health is broken because of my sins." The passage vividly describes the consequences of sin, such as festering wounds, pain, grief, and a sense of isolation. It highlights sin's toll on the body, emphasizing the need for healing and restoration.

In the New Testament, Jesus showed His ability to make sick people healthy, mend broken lives, and bring complete healing to those in pain. His mighty acts prove that He has control over physical sickness. According to Matthew 4:23-24 (NLT), Jesus traveled around Galilee, teaching in synagogues, spreading the Good News about the Kingdom, and healing all sorts of diseases and illnesses. The news about Him reached Syria, and people brought everyone unwell to Him. Whether they had different diseases, were possessed by demons, had seizures, or were paralyzed, Jesus healed them all.

Luke 6:17-19 (NLT) mentions that after coming down from a mountain, Jesus and His disciples were surrounded by a large crowd from places like Judea, Jerusalem, and even the coastal areas of Tyre and Sidon. People gathered to listen to Him and sought healing for their diseases. Those troubled by evil spirits found relief as well. Everyone wanted to touch Him because healing power radiated from Him, and He healed every person.
 By taking on our sins, Jesus provides a way for us to be restored and free from the consequences of wrongdoing, including physical illnesses. In Isaiah 53:4-5 (NLT), it's explained that Jesus carried our weaknesses and sorrows. Although some perceived his troubles as punishment for his sins, he endured suffering for our rebellion and was crushed for our wrongdoing. Through his sacrifice, we gain the opportunity for wholeness and healing.

1 Peter 2:24 (NLT) affirms that Jesus bore our sins on the cross so that we can be freed from sin and live according to what is right. The verse emphasizes that through his wounds, we find healing.

Crucially, faith plays a vital role in experiencing physical healing. It connects us with God's promises and opens us to receive His healing touch. The Bible stresses the significance of faith in divine healing. In Matthew 9:22 (NLT), Jesus attributes recovery to the woman's confidence, saying, "Daughter, be encouraged! Your faith has made you well." James 5:15 (NLT) further reinforces the power of faith in healing, stating that a prayer offered in faith will bring healing to the sick, and the Lord will restore health. Additionally, forgiveness is promised for any sins committed.

Recognizing the importance of faith, it's equally crucial to appreciate the value of medical care and a comprehensive approach to physical healing.

God has blessed healthcare professionals with knowledge and skills to assist in our journey to recovery. Combining medical interventions, making healthy lifestyle choices, and incorporating spiritual practices allow us to nurture our bodies and undergo healing.

In Luke 10:34-35 (NLT), we read about the Samaritan who cared for a wounded man, soothing his injuries with olive oil and wine, bandaging him, and ensuring he received further assistance at an inn. This illustrates the compatibility of compassionate care and physical healing.

Undoubtedly, physical healing is vital for our overall vitality and well-being. Understanding the link between sin and physical brokenness, recognizing Jesus as the ultimate source of healing, and embracing a holistic approach that integrates faith, medical care, and healthy practices enables us to experience restoration and wholeness.

The Impact of Chronic Stress and Worry on our Physical Health

Regarding our well-being, we can't overlook the harmful effects of long-lasting stress and worry. Continual pressure or ongoing anxiety can genuinely harm both our mental and physical health. Emphasis sets off the body's stress response, leading to physical and biological changes that can contribute to different illnesses and diseases. Here are ten examples of health conditions that can be linked to chronic stress:

- **Cardiovascular diseases**: Prolonged stress is a significant factor in the development of cardiovascular diseases, encompassing conditions like high blood pressure, heart disease, and an elevated risk of heart attacks or strokes. Stress is a natural reaction to challenging or threatening situations, yet it threatens the cardiovascular system when it becomes a persistent or overwhelming experience. Recognizing the link between stress and cardiovascular health is vital for implementing effective strategies to reduce these risks.

Extended exposure to stress triggers the body's stress response system, releasing hormones such as cortisol and adrenaline. These stress hormones increase blood pressure and heart rate, preparing the body for a fight-or-flight response. While this physiological reaction is beneficial in acute situations, the problem arises when chronic stress perpetuates these changes, leading to lasting damage to the cardiovascular system.

To delve deeper into how chronic stress impacts heart health, it is essential to consider the intricate interplay between the mind and body. The mind-body connection is dynamic in which mental and emotional states influence physical well-being. Chronic stress affects the body's immediate response and can contribute to unhealthy lifestyle choices. Individuals experiencing chronic stress may be more prone to engaging in behaviors such as overeating, smoking, or avoiding regular exercise – all of which are additional risk factors for cardiovascular diseases.

Furthermore, chronic stress can disrupt sleep patterns, compounding its detrimental effects on heart health. Quality sleep is integral to overall well-being, and its absence can exacerbate the negative impact of stress on the cardiovascular system.
Adequate rest allows the body to repair and regenerate, supporting optimal cardiovascular function.

In light of these considerations, adopting holistic stress management approaches becomes imperative for maintaining a healthy heart. Simple lifestyle changes, such as incorporating regular physical activity, practicing mindfulness techniques like deep breathing or meditation, and fostering strong social connections, can significantly alleviate chronic stress. Cultivating a positive mindset and prioritizing self-care are fundamental steps toward preserving cardiovascular health in facing life's challenges.

As the Bible wisely states in Philippians 4:6-7 (NIV), "Do not be anxious about anything, but in every situation, by prayer and petition, with thanksgiving, present your requests to God. And the peace of God, which transcends all understanding, will guard your hearts and minds in Christ Jesus." This timeless advice underscores the importance of finding peace amidst life's challenges, emphasizing the profound connection between mental well-being and heart health. When stress hormones remain consistently high, blood vessels narrow, making it more challenging for blood to move smoothly. This increases blood pressure, putting extra strain on the heart and potentially leading to heart disease and other complications.

Chronic stress impacts blood pressure and plays a role in atherosclerosis, where fatty deposits, known as plaques, accumulate inside arteries, reducing their diameter. These plaques can obstruct blood flow, raising the risk of blood clots and, consequently, heart attacks or strokes.

In the context of biblical teachings, the link between stress and cardiovascular health is illuminated by passages like Proverbs 12:25, which states, "Anxiety weighs down the heart, but a kind word cheers it up." The Bible underscores the significance of finding peace and trusting God's strength during stress and worry.

In the medical field, extensive research has firmly established the connection between chronic stress and cardiovascular diseases. Stress management techniques, including relaxation exercises, deep breathing, meditation, and engaging in emotionally uplifting activities, have proven effective in mitigating stress's impact on the cardiovascular system.

Moreover, embracing a healthy lifestyle, encompassing regular exercise, a balanced diet, and sufficient sleep, significantly contributes to cardiovascular well-being. Seeking social support, fostering connections with loved ones, and engaging in activities that bring joy and fulfillment can also play a crucial role in alleviating stress and reducing the risk of cardiovascular diseases.

Recognizing the signs of chronic stress is pivotal, and taking proactive steps to manage it is essential. Consulting healthcare professionals, such as doctors or therapists, can offer personalized guidance on stress management techniques and lifestyle adjustments to enhance cardiovascular health. By actively prioritizing stress reduction and adopting healthy coping strategies, individuals can safeguard their cardiovascular health and reduce the risk of heart disease, high blood pressure, and related conditions.

- **Digestive disorders:** Stress can have a profound impact on digestive health, worsening conditions such as irritable bowel syndrome (IBS), gastritis, ulcers, and inflammatory bowel disease. The connection between stress and digestive disorders is well-established, highlighting the importance of understanding and addressing this relationship for effective management and treatment.

The intricate interplay between stress and the digestive system is often called the "brain-gut axis." The body's stress response system kicks in when stress occurs, releasing hormones like cortisol. These stress hormones can influence the digestive system in various ways. One significant effect is the alteration of gut motility, which refers to the contractions of digestive muscles.

The stress-induced changes in gut motility can lead to increased or decreased movement in the digestive tract. For individuals dealing with conditions like IBS, these fluctuations in gut motility can worsen symptoms such as abdominal pain, bloating, diarrhea, or constipation.

Understanding the impact of stress on digestive health is essential for a comprehensive approach to managing these conditions. By recognizing the intricate connection between the mind and the digestive system, individuals can adopt strategies to mitigate stress and positively influence their overall well-being. Incorporating stress-reducing activities, such as mindfulness practices, regular exercise, and adequate sleep, can contribute to a healthier balance in the brain-gut axis.

In addition to lifestyle adjustments, seeking support from healthcare professionals is crucial for those managing digestive disorders exacerbated by stress. Medical interventions and personalized treatment plans can play a vital role in alleviating symptoms and improving the overall quality of life for individuals grappling with these challenging conditions.

Acknowledging and addressing the impact of stress on digestive health is a pivotal step in the journey towards effective management and treatment. By fostering a holistic approach that considers both physical and mental well-being, individuals can empower themselves to navigate the challenges posed by conditions like IBS, gastritis, ulcers, and inflammatory bowel disease.

Furthermore, stress affects our mental well-being and can significantly impact our physical health, particularly our digestive system. When stressed, the gut becomes more sensitive, making us more susceptible to pain and discomfort. This heightened sensitivity can exacerbate the symptoms of various digestive disorders, making them more pronounced and challenging to manage.

In addition to its effects on the gut, stress plays a role in compromising our immune system. This can lead to inflammation in the digestive tract, a particularly concerning process for individuals dealing with inflammatory bowel diseases like Crohn's disease and ulcerative colitis. These conditions involve chronic inflammation of the intestines, and prolonged stress can exacerbate this inflammation, triggering flare-ups and intensifying the overall disease activity.

Taking a moment to reflect on a biblical perspective, we find guidance on navigating stress and seeking peace in Philippians 4:6-7: "Do not be anxious about anything but in every situation, by prayer and petition, with thanksgiving, present your requests to God. And the peace of God, which transcends all understanding, will guard your hearts and minds in Christ Jesus." This scripture emphasizes the importance of praying, expressing gratitude, and seeking God's peace to alleviate anxiety and comfort in challenging situations. Incorporating such principles into our lives can be a valuable complement to managing stress and promoting overall well-being.

In medicine, numerous studies have highlighted how stress significantly affects digestive disorders. It's crucial to recognize that managing stress plays a pivotal role in alleviating symptoms related to digestive conditions. Simple techniques like relaxation exercises, mindfulness, and cognitive-behavioral therapy have proven effective in reducing stress-related symptoms in individuals grappling with digestive issues.

For a comprehensive approach to digestive health, embracing a healthy lifestyle becomes paramount. This involves a balanced diet, regular exercise, and adequate sleep. These lifestyle adjustments serve as foundational support for digestive well-being.

Making mindful dietary modifications can further enhance the management of digestive symptoms. Steering clear of trigger foods, moderating caffeine and alcohol intake, and incorporating fiber-rich foods into one's diet are practical steps toward digestive health.

In addition to lifestyle changes, seeking guidance from healthcare professionals is pivotal. Gastroenterologists and therapists can contribute significantly to developing a well-rounded treatment plan. They offer valuable insights into stress management techniques, prescribe necessary medications, and tailor their approach to address the specific needs of individuals grappling with digestive disorders.

Taking inspiration from the wisdom of the Bible, "Cast all your anxiety on him because he cares for you" (1 Peter 5:7), individuals are encouraged to lean on support systems, both professional and personal. By effectively managing stress and adopting a holistic approach to digestive health, individuals can alleviate symptoms and reduce inflammation, ultimately enhancing their overall well-being.

Prioritizing self-care is paramount. Seeking support, implementing strategies that promote relaxation, and focusing on emotional well-being are integral to managing stress-related digestive disorders effectively. By doing so, individuals embark on a journey towards a healthier and more balanced life.

- **Respiratory problems**: Stress significantly impacts respiratory health, particularly for individuals with asthma and respiratory diseases. The connection between stress and respiratory issues is well-established, with stress exacerbating symptoms and increasing the likelihood of respiratory infections.

Asthma, a chronic inflammatory condition affecting the airways, is susceptible to stress. When people encounter stress, their body activates the stress response system, releasing hormones like cortisol. These hormones can initiate inflammation and constrict the airways, making breathing more challenging for asthma patients.

Furthermore, stress can contribute to asthma attacks by triggering the release of histamine and other substances. These compounds can further constrict the airways and heighten inflammation, intensifying the impact of stress on respiratory health. It's crucial to recognize that stress doesn't just stop at symptom aggravation; it can also compromise the immune system.

Stress weakens the immune system's defenses, rendering individuals more susceptible to respiratory infections. This heightened vulnerability to diseases can, in turn, worsen asthma symptoms, creating a cycle of increased respiratory distress. It underscores the importance of managing stress for symptom relief and bolsters the overall respiratory well-being of individuals with asthma and respiratory diseases.

The intricate interplay between stress and respiratory health emphasizes the need for comprehensive approaches to managing conditions like asthma. By addressing stress and its impact on the respiratory system, individuals can take proactive steps to improve their overall well-being and minimize the risk of exacerbated symptoms and respiratory infections.

The scriptures highlight the importance of finding peace and trust in God during times of stress in Psalm 56:3 (NLT): "When I am afraid, I put my trust in you." This verse encourages us to entrust our worries to God, seeking comfort and alleviating anxiety, ultimately positively affecting our respiratory health.

From a medical perspective, numerous studies underscore a connection between stress and asthma exacerbations. Managing stress through simple techniques like deep breathing exercises, relaxation methods, and meditation has proven effective in alleviating stress-related symptoms in individuals with asthma. These practices contribute to emotional well-being and positively impact respiratory health.

It's crucial to recognize that stress reduction extends beyond asthma management. Stress weakens the immune system, heightening susceptibility to viral and bacterial infections. This vulnerability is particularly noteworthy in respiratory conditions like asthma. By adopting stress management strategies, individuals can fortify their immune systems, reducing the risk of respiratory infections. The common cold and influenza, both triggered by viral infections, can exacerbate symptoms in those with respiratory conditions.

The wisdom from Psalm 56:3 aligns with spiritual and medical insights, emphasizing the interconnectedness of finding solace in faith and implementing practical stress-reduction measures for overall well-being. As we navigate life's challenges, the union of trust in God and adopting stress-relieving practices can pave the way for a healthier and more resilient life. Implementing strategies to manage stress and boost the immune system is crucial for reducing the risk of respiratory infections and lessening their impact on respiratory health. Maintaining a healthy lifestyle is essential by incorporating regular exercise, ensuring proper nutrition, getting sufficient sleep, and avoiding smoking or exposure to secondhand smoke. These measures enhance overall well-being and play a significant role in supporting respiratory function.

To delve deeper into stress management, consider incorporating relaxation techniques such as deep breathing exercises, meditation, or yoga into your routine. These practices have been shown to reduce stress levels, positively affecting the immune system. A calm and relaxed mind can contribute to better respiratory health.

Additionally, paying attention to your diet is vital. Include a variety of fruits, vegetables, and whole grains in your meals to provide essential nutrients that support immune function. Hydration is equally important, so make sure to drink an adequate amount of water throughout the day.

Furthermore, maintaining a consistent sleep schedule can significantly impact stress levels and immune function. Aim for 7-9 hours of quality sleep each night to allow your body the necessary time to repair and regenerate. Lack of sleep can weaken the immune system, making you more susceptible to respiratory infections.

Avoiding smoking and secondhand smoke is a fundamental aspect of respiratory health. The chemicals in smoke can damage the lungs and impair their ability to function correctly. If you are a smoker, seeking support to quit can be a pivotal step in improving your respiratory well-being.

A holistic approach to health by addressing stress, maintaining a nutritious diet, ensuring sufficient sleep, and avoiding harmful substances like tobacco smoke can significantly bolster your immune system and promote optimal respiratory function. As the Bible wisely says in Proverbs 17:22 (NIV), "A cheerful heart is a good medicine, but a crushed spirit dries up the bones." Indeed, a positive and balanced approach to life can profoundly affect mental and physical well-being.

Seeking advice from healthcare experts, like pulmonologists or allergists, is vital for handling stress-related respiratory conditions. These professionals can create personalized treatment plans, recommend suitable medications, and suggest stress management techniques tailored to individuals, aiding them in better dealing with their symptoms.
Effectively managing stress and incorporating stress-reduction practices can significantly reduce the impact of stress on respiratory health. Prioritizing self-care, maintaining a healthy lifestyle, and obtaining support from healthcare professionals are vital steps to alleviate symptoms, enhance lung function, and improve overall respiratory well-being.

In addition, fostering a supportive environment and open communication with friends and family can contribute to better stress management. Exploring relaxation techniques, such as deep breathing exercises or mindfulness meditation, can be valuable in promoting a sense of calm and reducing the physiological effects of stress on the respiratory system.
Moreover, staying physically active is beneficial for both mental and respiratory health. Engaging in regular exercise not only helps in stress reduction but also contributes to improved lung function and overall well-

being. Choosing activities that suit individual preferences and physical capabilities is essential to ensure consistency in maintaining an active lifestyle.

Collaborating with healthcare professionals, adopting stress management techniques, fostering a supportive social environment, and incorporating regular physical activity are integral components of a holistic approach to managing stress-related respiratory conditions. As the Bible reminds us in Philippians 4:6-7 (NIV), "Do not be anxious about anything, but in every situation, by prayer and petition, with thanksgiving, present your requests to God. And the peace of God, which transcends all understanding, will guard your hearts and minds in Christ Jesus."

- **Weakened immune system:** Chronic stress takes a toll on the immune system, making people more prone to infections, autoimmune issues, and slower healing of wounds. It significantly affects the body's defense mechanism, leaving it vulnerable to illnesses and delayed injury recovery.

Our immune system is like a vigilant guardian, identifying and eliminating harmful invaders like bacteria and viruses. It's a complex network of cells, tissues, and organs working harmoniously to keep the body safe. However, chronic stress disrupts this harmony. When stress becomes a constant companion, it throws the immune system off balance.

Stress sets off the body's stress response, unleashing stress hormones like cortisol. In the short term, focus can boost immune function, but it takes a toll when prolonged. Continuous exposure to elevated cortisol levels can suppress the immune system, impairing its ability to fend off pathogens effectively.

Think of the immune system as a well-orchestrated team and chronic stress as a disruptive force that throws the unit off. In trying to cope with stress, the body inadvertently weakens its defenses. This weakening of the immune system can lead to a heightened susceptibility to infections and a slower wound-healing process.

So, it's not just a matter of feeling mentally drained when stressed; the impact extends to the very core of our physical well-being. It's a reminder of the intricate connection between our mental and physical health. Taking steps to manage stress isn't just a luxury; it's crucial to maintaining overall health and resilience. The Bible wisely notes in Proverbs 17:22, "A joyful heart is a good medicine, but a crushed spirit dries up the bones." Indeed, nurturing our mental and physical well-being is a holistic prescription for a healthier and more resilient life.

The Word of God underscores the vital role of managing stress and anxiety for maintaining good health. Philippians 4:6-7(NIV) counsels, "Do not be anxious about anything, but in every situation, by prayer and petition, with thanksgiving, present your requests to God.

And the peace of God, which transcends all understanding, will guard your hearts and minds in Christ Jesus." This biblical passage highlights the importance of turning to God during times of stress and discovering peace through prayer and trust.

In addition to seeking spiritual solace, it is imperative to implement practical strategies that contribute to overall well-being and immune system strength. Embracing stress management techniques becomes crucial in mitigating the adverse effects of chronic stress. Incorporating mindfulness, meditation, and deep breathing exercises into your routine can significantly alleviate stress. Moreover, engaging in activities that foster relaxation and emotional well-being, such as spending quality time with loved ones, pursuing hobbies, or enjoying nature, enhances the effectiveness of stress management.

Remember that caring for your mental and emotional health intertwines with physical well-being. You can strive towards a balanced and resilient life by cultivating a holistic approach to health, incorporating both spiritual and practical elements. This integrated approach aligns with biblical wisdom and resonates with the contemporary understanding of holistic well-being.

Maintaining a robust immune system is crucial for overall well-being. To achieve this, it's essential to adopt a healthy lifestyle. Start by incorporating a well-rounded diet of fruits, vegetables, and nutrients that support your immune system. Regular exercise is equally essential, as it keeps your body fit and contributes to a more robust defense against illnesses.

Quality sleep is another critical component of a healthy lifestyle. Ensure you get enough restorative sleep each night, as it plays a significant role in immune function. Avoiding habits that can compromise your immune system, such as smoking and excessive alcohol consumption, is also vital. These simple lifestyle changes contribute to building a strong and resilient immune system.

If you find yourself grappling with chronic stress, it's crucial to seek support from healthcare professionals. Reach out to primary care physicians or immunologists who can offer valuable guidance on managing the impact of stress on your immune system. They can provide personalized recommendations tailored to your specific needs. Sometimes, they prescribe treatments or medications to address underlying issues and monitor your overall immune health.

Taking proactive steps to address and manage chronic stress can yield numerous benefits.

Strengthening your immune system becomes a tangible outcome, reducing the risk of infections and improving your ability to manage autoimmune disorders. Additionally, enhancing your body's capacity to heal and recover becomes more attainable with effective stress management.
Embracing a healthy lifestyle, seeking guidance from healthcare professionals, and actively managing chronic stress are integral elements in fortifying your immune system. As the Bible wisely reminds us, "Beloved, I pray that all may go well with you and that you may be in good health, as it goes well with your soul" (3 John 1:2, ESV). These steps promote physical health, well-being, and a more fulfilling life.

- **Chronic pain:** Stress doesn't just affect our minds; it can also make physical pain feel more intense. This heightened pain perception can lead to various issues like tension headaches, migraines, and conditions like fibromyalgia. Imagine trying to go about your daily life, but even simple activities become a challenge because of chronic pain. Millions of people around the world face this reality.

What's interesting is that stress isn't just a bystander in this scenario—it plays a significant role in how we experience and feel chronic pain. When we're stressed, whether because of things happening around us or concerns within ourselves, our bodies release stress hormones such as cortisol and adrenaline. These hormones don't just prepare us for a "fight or flight" response; they also crank up our sensitivity to pain and make discomfort feel more pronounced.

This link between stress and pain isn't just a coincidence. It's like pressure turns up the volume on our pain signals, making the pain harder to ignore. So, managing stress isn't just about keeping a clear head; it's also about easing the physical burden that stress can place on our bodies. By understanding this connection, we can take steps to not only alleviate stress but also reduce the impact it has on our experience of chronic pain. It's about finding a balance that allows us to navigate life more efficiently and with less discomfort. As the Bible wisely says, "Come to me, all you who are weary and burdened, and I will give you rest" (Matthew 11:28, NIV). Taking a moment to find that rest might be a critical step in managing both stress and chronic pain in our lives.

In the biblical context, Psalm 55:22 (NIV) encourages people to trust the Lord for support, stating, "Cast your cares on the LORD, and he will sustain you; he will never let the righteous be shaken." This verse emphasizes the significance of relying on God's strength and finding solace in Him during challenging times.

Looking at stress-induced pain from a medical standpoint reveals its intricate nature, involving various physiological and psychological processes. Stress has the potential to cause muscle tension, which can contribute to tension headaches and migraines. Furthermore, stress can trigger the body's inflammatory response, leading to the release of inflammatory molecules that intensify pain perception and may contribute to conditions such as fibromyalgia.

Understanding the wisdom in the biblical verse, we see a connection between casting our burdens upon the Lord and alleviating the burdensome effects of stress-induced pain.

By seeking comfort in God, we open ourselves to a source of strength beyond our own, fostering resilience in the face of life's challenges.

It's important to acknowledge that while the biblical perspective provides spiritual guidance, seeking professional help for managing stress and its physical manifestations is equally crucial. Combining faith with practical strategies, such as mindfulness and relaxation techniques, can create a holistic approach to well-being. Taking steps to care for both our spiritual and physical selves enhances our ability to navigate the complexities of life with grace and resilience
.

The biblical guidance in Psalm 55:22 encourages us to turn to God for strength during times of stress, complementing our understanding of stress-induced pain from a medical viewpoint. Integrating faith and practical strategies can contribute to a balanced and resilient approach to well-being, allowing us to face life's challenges with a fortified spirit and a healthier body.

Psychologically, stress has the potential to heighten feelings of anxiety and depression, thereby intensifying the manifestation of pain symptoms. The intricate interplay between the mind and body significantly influences the perception of pain, with stress acting as an amplifier for the psychological distress linked to chronic pain. Effectively managing chronic pain necessitates a comprehensive strategy that encompasses both physical and emotional dimensions. Consider implementing the following procedures to enhance your approach:

- **Stress Management Techniques**

Stress management is crucial for maintaining overall well-being, and incorporating various techniques into your routine can significantly enhance your ability to cope with stressors. One practical approach involves engaging in stress reduction practices such as mindfulness meditation, deep breathing exercises, and relaxation techniques.

- **Mindfulness Meditation**: This stress management technique, for instance, encourages you to be fully present in the moment, fostering a sense of awareness that can mitigate the impact of stress on both your mind and body. Dedicating time to mindfulness creates a mental space to observe and acknowledge stressors without becoming overwhelmed.

Deep breathing exercises play a pivotal role in reducing stress by promoting the nervous system's relaxation. By taking slow, deep breaths, you activate the body's parasympathetic response, countering the physiological effects of stress. Incorporating these exercises into your daily routine can cultivate a habit of calmness, making it easier to manage stress as it arises.

Additionally, exploring various relaxation techniques, such as progressive muscle relaxation or guided imagery, can offer diverse tools for stress management. Progressive muscle relaxation involves systematically tensing and then relaxing different muscle groups, promoting a release of physical tension.
Guided imagery uses visualization to create a calming mental space, diverting your focus from stressors.

Consistency is critical when incorporating these stress management techniques into your lifestyle. By making them a regular part of your routine, you build resilience over time, enhancing your capacity to handle stress and reducing the overall intensity of pain associated with it. Remember that stress management is a holistic endeavor, and finding a combination of techniques that resonate with you can contribute to a more comprehensive and practical approach to stress reduction.

- **Physical therapy and exercise:** Physical therapy and exercise enhance overall physical well-being. Collaborating with a skilled physical therapist or participating in personalized low-impact exercises can significantly improve flexibility, strength, and overall physical function. These tailored exercises consider individual capabilities, ensuring a safe and effective approach to rehabilitation and fitness.

Furthermore, the benefits extend beyond the physical realm. Regular engagement in physical activity has been shown to release endorphins, the body's natural pain-relieving chemicals. This helps alleviate discomfort and improves mood and overall mental well-being.

Incorporating a diverse range of exercises into a routine can target different muscle groups, promoting a well-rounded approach to physical fitness. This includes stretching for flexibility, strength training for muscle development, and cardiovascular exercises for heart health. A comprehensive exercise plan ensures that various aspects of physical function are addressed, leading to a more holistic improvement in overall well-being.

It's essential to emphasize the importance of consistency in physical therapy and exercise routines. Regular, ongoing participation in these activities is critical to sustaining the positive effects on flexibility, strength, and mental health. Moreover, the guidance of a knowledgeable physical therapist can help individuals adapt and progress their exercises over time, ensuring continued improvement and preventing plateaus in physical function.

In conclusion, targeted physical therapy and a well-rounded exercise routine tailored to individual capabilities can significantly enhance flexibility, strength, and overall physical function. The added benefit of endorphin release contributes not only to pain relief but also to an improved mood and mental well-being. Consistency in these activities, guided by a professional when needed, is vital for sustaining these positive effects over the long term.

- **Pain medication and interventions:** Pain management strategies encompass a spectrum of approaches tailored to the discomfort's intensity and root cause. Healthcare professionals employ various tools, ranging from pharmaceutical interventions to procedural techniques, to address pain symptoms effectively.

Medications play a pivotal role in pain management. Nonsteroidal anti-inflammatory drugs (NSAIDs) are commonly prescribed to alleviate pain and reduce inflammation. Opioids, another class of medications, may be considered in cases of moderate to severe pain, albeit with careful monitoring due to potential side effects and dependency concerns. These pharmaceutical interventions are often chosen based on the nature and severity of the pain, with healthcare providers customizing their recommendations to suit individual patient needs.

In addition to medications, interventional procedures represent a crucial facet of pain management. Healthcare professionals may recommend nerve blocks or other targeted interventions designed to address the specific underlying cause of the pain. Nerve blocks involve injecting anesthetic or anti-inflammatory medications directly into or around nerves, disrupting pain signals and providing relief. These procedures are precious in cases where pinpointing the source of pain allows for a more targeted and practical approach to symptom management.

Furthermore, a comprehensive pain management plan may involve a multidisciplinary approach, incorporating physical therapy, psychological support, and lifestyle modifications. Physical therapy can enhance flexibility and strength, promoting overall well-being and potentially reducing pain. Psychological support, such as cognitive-behavioral therapy, can assist individuals in coping with chronic pain by addressing the emotional and mental aspects associated with their condition. Lifestyle modifications, including exercise, proper nutrition, and stress management, may contribute to long-term pain relief and improved quality of life.

In summary, pain management extends beyond a singular approach, encompassing a range of medications, interventional procedures, and holistic strategies. Tailoring these interventions to patients' needs ensures a comprehensive and practical approach to pain relief.

- **Support networks and counseling:** Building a robust support system is crucial for individuals grappling with chronic pain. Connecting with family and friends, participating in support groups, and engaging in open conversations can provide profound emotional support and understanding. Additionally, seeking professional counseling or therapy is a valuable step in navigating the complex emotional and psychological dimensions of chronic pain.

In addition to seeking support, addressing stress is pivotal in managing chronic pain effectively. Incorporating comprehensive pain management strategies into one's daily routine can significantly alleviate the impact of persistent pain on overall well-being. Collaborating closely with healthcare professionals is critical to developing a personalized treatment plan that combines medical interventions, stress management techniques, and psychological support.

It's essential to recognize that chronic pain not only affects the physical aspect of an individual's life but also takes a toll on their mental and emotional well-being. Integrating psychological support into the treatment plan helps individuals understand and cope with the emotional challenges associated with chronic pain.

Individuals can gradually regain control over their pain through consistent efforts, patience, and perseverance. This process involves a holistic approach encompassing medical, emotional, and psychological aspects. By taking these steps, individuals can enhance their quality of life, mitigate the impact of chronic pain on their daily activities, and improve their overall well-being over time.

- **Sleep Disorders and Stress**: The intricate relationship between stress and sleep disruption is well-documented, with pressure acting as a significant catalyst for various sleep disorders such as insomnia, restless leg syndrome, and sleep apnea. Recognizing the profound importance of sleep in sustaining overall health and well-being, it becomes crucial to delve deeper into the impact of prolonged stress on sleep patterns and the subsequent development of sleep disorders.

Insomnia, a prevalent sleep disorder, manifests as challenges in falling asleep, staying asleep, or achieving restorative sleep. The harmful effects of stress and worry are undeniable contributors to insomnia, fostering racing thoughts that hinder relaxation and impede restful sleep. The biblical passage in Psalm 4:8(NIV) beautifully captures the essence of finding solace amidst stress, stating, "In peace, I will lie down and sleep, for you alone, LORD, make me dwell in safety." This verse underscores the significance of seeking tranquility and security in the divine, offering a potential pathway to alleviate stress and foster improved sleep quality.

Understanding the multifaceted nature of sleep disorders associated with anxiety provides valuable insights into the intricate interplay between mental and physical well-being. Delving into additional facets of stress-induced sleep disturbances, such as restless leg syndrome and sleep apnea, further enriches our comprehension of the complexities involved. By acknowledging these nuances, we can better appreciate the holistic impact of stress on sleep and, subsequently, on an individual's overall health.

In conclusion, the profound connection between stress and sleep disorders necessitates a comprehensive approach to mitigate their effects. Exploring coping mechanisms, adopting relaxation techniques, and, as highlighted in the biblical reference, finding solace in a higher power are integral to promoting a healthy balance between stress management and optimal sleep.

Restless Leg Syndrome (RLS) is a sleep disorder characterized by an irresistible urge to move the legs, accompanied by discomfort. Stress further complicates this condition, rendering it challenging for individuals to attain restful sleep. To delve deeper into the intricacies of RLS, it's crucial to understand the multifaceted impact of stress on the disorder.

Sleep apnea, another prevalent condition, involves repetitive breathing interruptions during sleep. Stress is a catalyst for this disorder, causing the muscles in the throat and airway to tense, leading to partial or complete blockage. Consequently, interrupted breathing results in fragmented sleep and diminished oxygen levels in the body. The interplay between stress and sleep disorders becomes apparent through these physiological mechanisms.

The complex relationship between stress and sleep disorders extends to hormonal responses. Stress induces the release of hormones like cortisol, disrupting the natural sleep-wake cycle. Additionally, stress activates the sympathetic nervous system, elevating heart rate, blood pressure, and alertness, all interfering with sleep. This intricate web of physiological responses underscores the importance of addressing stress as a central factor in sleep-related issues.

On a psychological level, stress contributes to anxiety, racing thoughts, and persistent worry, creating a barrier to relaxation and sleep initiation. The ensuing compromised sleep quality intensifies pressure, establishing a detrimental cycle that perpetuates sleep disorders.

A comprehensive approach is essential to effectively tackle stress-related sleep disorders, targeting both the root stressors and the resultant sleep disturbances. Implementing strategies to foster better sleep is imperative in breaking the cycle of stress-induced sleep disorders. Here are some enhanced strategies to promote restful sleep:

Exploring and utilizing stress management through proven techniques like mindfulness meditation, deep breathing exercises, and journaling is very helpful. These practices promote mental tranquillity and physical relaxation, creating an optimal pre-bedtime routine. Embrace mindfulness to quiet the mind, engage in deep breathing for profound peace, and capture thoughts in a journal for emotional release. Incorporating these strategies into your routine fosters a serene mental state and enhances overall well-being.

- **Establishing a bedtime routine:** Crafting a bedtime routine is crucial for signaling your body that it's time to unwind and prepare for sleep. Ensure consistency in your pre-sleep pattern, incorporating activities like a relaxing warm bath, indulging in a good book, or immersing yourself in soothing music. Establishing these habits creates a conducive environment for a restful night, promoting better sleep quality and overall well-being.

- **Sleep hygiene practices:** Optimal sleep hygiene is essential for quality rest. Ensure your bedroom is dark, calm, and quiet, steering clear of stimulating activities and screens before bedtime. Maintaining a consistent sleep schedule aids in establishing a healthy sleep routine. Additionally, Cognitive-Behavioral Therapy for Insomnia (CBT-I) proves effective in addressing negative thought patterns and behaviors linked to sleep troubles. This therapeutic approach emphasizes enhancing sleep habits and incorporating relaxation techniques, fostering a holistic approach to tackling insomnia.

- **Seeking medical evaluation:** Consulting a healthcare professional is crucial for persistent sleep issues. They can assess and diagnose underlying sleep disorders, recommending tailored treatments like medication or specialized therapies. By tackling stress and adopting healthy sleep habits, individuals can enhance sleep quality and duration, promoting overall physical and mental well-being. Prioritizing sleep as a fundamental aspect of self-care is vital

Seeking professional help ensures optimal sleep health and a comprehensive approach to addressing underlying issues.

- **Mental health disorders**: Chronic stress significantly amplifies the risk of mental health disorders, fostering the development or escalation of anxiety, depression, and various other psychological conditions. Persistent stressors strain the mind, creating a conducive environment for these disorders to manifest. Proactively managing stress through mindfulness, therapy, or lifestyle adjustments becomes pivotal in cultivating mental well-being. Addressing the root causes and adopting coping mechanisms can mitigate the impact of chronic stress, empowering individuals to navigate life's challenges with resilience and promoting a healthier mental state.

- **Weight gain and obesity**: Chronic stress poses a considerable threat to our health, fostering overeating and poor food decisions that contribute to weight gain and obesity. This perilous link between stress and unhealthy eating habits can lead to severe health issues. Stress disrupts our dietary patterns, promoting overindulgence in unhealthy foods, thereby escalating the risk of obesity-related complications. Understanding the intricate connection between stress and our relationship with food is vital in addressing and mitigating the adverse impact on weight. Exploring these dynamics to manage stress-induced weight gain and prioritize overall well-being proactively is crucial.

- **Emotional eating:** Eating can respond to chronic stress and manifests as a coping mechanism through food. This behavior involves using food to manage or suppress negative emotions triggered by stress-induced hormones like cortisol. This often leads to heightened cravings for sugary, fatty, and calorie-dense foods. The consequence may be excessive consumption, contributing to gradual weight gain. Understanding and addressing emotional eating is crucial for fostering a healthier relationship with food and managing the impact of stress on dietary habits.

- **Unhealthy food choices:** When faced with stress, individuals often gravitate towards convenient food options rich in calories, unhealthy fats, and sugars. While these choices may offer momentary comfort and stress relief, they typically lack the vital nutrients essential for optimal health. Repeatedly opting for such unhealthy foods can lead to weight gain and elevate the likelihood of developing obesity-related health concerns, including diabetes, heart disease, and specific types of cancers. It is crucial to be mindful of these dietary patterns and make informed choices to support overall well-being.

- **Hormonal changes**: Prolonged stress can disturb the delicate equilibrium of hormones in appetite regulation. Cortisol, the primary stress hormone, exerts influence over the metabolism of carbohydrates, fats, and proteins, potentially resulting in weight gain and heightened fat accumulation in the abdominal area. Beyond cortisol, stress can also impact other vital hormones like insulin and leptin, which are crucial in controlling appetite and satiety. The disruption of these hormonal dynamics may pave the way for overeating and subsequent weight gain. Understanding and addressing these hormonal imbalances is essential for effective weight management strategies.

- **Lack of Physical Activity**: The influence of stress extends beyond mere emotional strain; it also detrimentally affects our motivation and vitality, posing a formidable barrier to regular physical activity. This diminished activity level not only curtails calorie expenditure but also becomes a significant factor contributing to weight gain. Additionally, the persistent pressures of chronic stress can impede individuals from adhering to consistent exercise routines, thereby limiting opportunities for effective weight management and overall well-being. The repercussions of weight gain stemming from prolonged stress create a self-perpetuating cycle. Elevated body weight, coupled with dissatisfaction, fosters heightened anxiety and emotional distress, fostering unhealthy eating patterns and further weight gain. Breaking free from this detrimental loop necessitates addressing the root stressors and cultivating healthier coping mechanisms.

It is crucial to recognize that combating stress-induced weight gain and obesity demands a comprehensive approach, one that seamlessly integrates biblical, medical, and psychological principles. Below are strategic measures to effectively manage stress-related weight gain and cultivate enduring healthy habits:

- **Stress Management Techniques:** Incorporating stress-reduction activities into your routine, such as regular exercise, practicing meditation or prayer, and embracing mindfulness, can significantly alleviate stress. These proactive measures not only address the immediate symptoms of anxiety but also serve to diminish emotional eating triggers, promoting overall well-being.

- **Optimal Nutrition:** Strive for a well-rounded diet emphasizing whole, unprocessed foods abundant in vital nutrients. Elevate your plate with a colorful array of fruits, vegetables, lean proteins, whole grains, and nourishing fats while minimizing the consumption of sugary snacks, processed foods, and detrimental fats.

- **Mindful Culinary Habits:** Embrace mindful eating by attuning yourself to hunger and fullness signals, relishing each bite, and fostering a profound connection with your meals. This cautious approach nurtures a healthier relationship with food and acts as a bulwark against overindulgence.

- **Regular Physical Engagement:** Infuse your routine with consistent physical activity to bolster weight management, alleviate stress, uplift mood, and enhance overall well-being. Opt for activities that bring you joy, seamlessly integrating them into your lifestyle for sustained benefits.

- **Seeking Professional Support:** When the burden of stress-related weight gain becomes too heavy, consider contacting healthcare professionals, registered dietitians, or therapists. Their expertise can furnish valuable guidance, instill accountability, and tailor personalized strategies to address the root causes of stress and align with your weight management goals.

By confronting the impact of stress on weight gain and adopting these wholesome lifestyle habits, individuals can embark on a journey to uphold a healthy weight. This proactive approach mitigates the risk of obesity-related health issues and contributes to holistic well-being.

- **Skin conditions**: Chronic stress can profoundly impact skin health by exacerbating conditions such as eczema, psoriasis, acne, and hives. Stress catalyzes heightened symptoms and contributes to developing or worsening these skin issues. Delving into the intricate relationship between stress and skin conditions reveals a noteworthy connection. Eczema, psoriasis, acne, and hives can all intensify under persistent stress. Understanding how stress affects the skin is crucial for comprehensive skincare. This interconnected dynamic emphasizes the importance of stress management in maintaining healthy skin. By addressing stressors, individuals can proactively mitigate the impact on their skin, fostering a holistic approach to skincare that considers both physical and emotional well-being.

- **Eczema:** Eczema, or atopic dermatitis, is a chronic inflammatory skin condition characterized by red, itchy, and dry patches. Stress emerges as a key player in triggering or intensifying eczema symptoms. It does so by amplifying inflammation and worsening skin irritation. The impact of stress hormones, particularly cortisol, on the immune system is profound. This disruption compromises the skin's natural barrier function, rendering it more susceptible to allergens and irritants, fueling eczema's progression.

- **Psoriasis:** Psoriasis is a chronic autoimmune skin condition characterized by the rapid turnover of skin cells, resulting in thick, red, and scaly patches. Stress can contribute to the onset or exacerbation of psoriasis symptoms. The exact mechanism is not fully understood, but stress is believed to trigger immune system responses and inflammation, leading to the flare-up of psoriatic lesions. Acne is a common skin condition characterized by pimples, blackheads, and whiteheads. While hormonal factors primarily influence acne, chronic stress can worsen acne symptoms. Stress triggers the release of stress hormones, which can stimulate the production of sebum (skin oil) and increase inflammation, contributing to clogged pores and the development of acne.

- **Hives (Urticaria):** Hives, or urticaria, are raised, itchy welts on the skin that can appear suddenly and disappear within hours. Stress is a common trigger for hives, and emotional stress can lead to the release of substances like histamine, causing blood vessels to leak and resulting in packs.

Chronic stress can make individuals more susceptible to recurrent episodes of hives.

The connection between stress and skin conditions is multifaceted, involving various physiological and biological processes:

- **Inflammation:** Chronic stress triggers the body's stress response, heightening inflammation. This elevated inflammation adversely affects the entire body, exacerbating pre-existing skin conditions and hindering the skin's inherent healing mechanisms. Addressing chronic stress is crucial for maintaining skin health, as unchecked inflammation can impede the body's ability to recover naturally.

- **Immune System Dysregulation**: Prolonged stress disrupts the immune system, triggering an overactive or imbalanced response. This dysregulation significantly heightens the risk of developing or exacerbating autoimmune-related skin conditions, such as psoriasis. Stress management is pivotal in maintaining immune equilibrium and mitigating the impact on skin health.

- **Hormonal Imbalance**: Stress initiates the release of cortisol, a stress hormone that can disrupt hormone equilibrium in the body. This hormonal imbalance may adversely impact sebum production and the turnover of skin cells, thereby exacerbating the occurrence of acne breakouts. Addressing stress is essential not only for mental well-being but also for maintaining healthier skin. By managing stress levels, individuals can mitigate the impact of cortisol on hormonal fluctuations, promoting more transparent and more balanced skin.

- **Skin Barrier Function:** Stress can weaken the skin's protective barrier, heightening vulnerability to irritants, allergens, and moisture depletion, thereby intensifying symptoms of eczema and other skin conditions. Effectively managing stress and its repercussions on the skin requires a holistic approach that combines biblical, medical, and psychological principles. This multifaceted strategy aims to restore the skin's resilience by fostering a balance between spiritual well-being, medical interventions, and mental health practices. In doing so, it endeavors to fortify the skin's natural defenses and mitigate the adverse effects of stress, promoting overall skin health and alleviating conditions associated with its compromised state. Here are some strategies to manage stress and promote skin health:

- **Stress Management:** Incorporate stress-reducing practices into your routine, such as deep breathing exercises, meditation, prayer, or relaxing hobbies. Effectively managing stress fosters overall well-being and minimizes its adverse effects on the skin. Prioritize self-care through these techniques to cultivate a healthier mind-body balance, promoting a radiant and resilient complexion.

SKINCARE ROUTINE:
1. Cultivate a gentle and steadfast skincare regimen by selecting products tailored to your skin's needs.
2. Steer clear of harsh cleansers and abrasive treatments, as these can exacerbate skin irritation.
3. Choose mild, soothing alternatives to nurture your skin.

Consistency is critical to maintaining a healthy complexion. Embrace a routine that promotes balance and avoids unnecessary stress on your skin. Prioritize products that align with your skin type, fostering a harmonious and radiant glow.

- **Healthy Lifestyle Habits:** Embrace a health-focused lifestyle by prioritizing regular exercise, ample sleep, and a well-rounded diet. Cultivating these habits fosters holistic well-being, positively impacting skin health. Consistent physical activity enhances circulation, promoting a radiant complexion, while sufficient sleep aids cell regeneration, contributing to a youthful appearance. A balanced diet rich in nutrients ensures skin vitality, reflecting overall health. Elevate your quality of life by incorporating these habits into your routine, empowering your well-being and promoting a vibrant and glowing complexion.

- **Seek Professional Guidance:** Consult dermatologists to receive tailored treatments, medications, or therapies to manage various skin conditions properly. Complement dermatological care by consulting mental health professionals to tackle underlying stressors and cultivate efficient coping mechanisms. Understanding the profound connection between stress and skin health empowers individuals to adopt targeted strategies, fostering improved skin and overall well-being. Embrace a holistic approach that encompasses physical, emotional, and spiritual dimensions of healing for a more balanced and healthier life. Integrating these expert insights ensures a comprehensive and proactive approach to skincare, optimizing the potential for long-term positive outcomes. Prioritize your skin health by recognizing the interconnected nature of physical and emotional well-being and taking deliberate steps towards a more harmonious and fulfilling lifestyle.

- **Reproductive problems**: Chronic stress can impact reproductive health, leading to menstrual irregularities, decreased fertility, and sexual dysfunction. Chronic stress can influence reproductive issues, affecting men and women in various ways. Prolonged stress can disrupt the delicate balance of hormones and physiological processes involved in reproductive health, leading to menstrual irregularities, decreased fertility, and sexual dysfunction. Let's explore how chronic stress can affect the reproductive system and contribute to these issues.

- **Menstrual Irregularities**: Stress, when persistent, profoundly impacts reproductive health in both men and women. The enduring burden disrupts the delicate balance of hormonal regulation and physiological processes crucial for reproductive well-being. This disruption manifests in menstrual irregularities, diminished fertility, and sexual dysfunction. By delving into the intricate relationship between chronic stress and reproductive health, we uncover the multifaceted impact on the mechanisms orchestrating fertility and sexual function in both genders. Understanding these dynamics is pivotal in devising strategies to mitigate the adverse effects of chronic stress on the reproductive system, fostering a comprehensive approach to health and well-being. As we navigate the complex interplay between stressors and reproductive well-being, it becomes clear that addressing chronic stress is integral to promoting a healthier and more balanced reproductive system.

- **Decreased Fertility**: Prolonged stress significantly influences fertility in both genders. For women, stress disrupts ovulation, posing challenges to conception. Moreover, it hampers the uterine environment, diminishing its receptivity to implantation. In men, pressure exerts adverse effects on sperm production, motility, and quality, thereby lowering the likelihood of successful fertilization. Acknowledging these interconnected aspects of reproductive health underscores the importance of stress management in optimizing fertility. Implementing stress-reduction techniques, such as mindfulness, exercise, and adequate sleep, becomes paramount for couples navigating the complexities of conception. Striking a balance in mental well-being can positively impact reproductive processes, fostering an environment conducive to achieving the shared goal of parenthood.

- **Sexual Dysfunction**: Chronic stress can significantly impact sexual function in both men and women. In women, stress may manifest as reduced libido, vaginal dryness, and challenges in achieving orgasm. Men, on the other hand, may experience erectile dysfunction or premature ejaculation due to stress. These issues arise from the intricate interplay of chronic stress with the endocrine system, central nervous system, and psychological factors. The physiological and psychological repercussions of pressure can disrupt the delicate balance necessary for sexual desire and pleasure. Understanding the multifaceted impact of chronic stress on reproductive health is crucial, as it involves intricate connections between various bodily systems and psychological elements. By recognizing and addressing these complexities, individuals can take proactive steps to mitigate the adverse effects of stress on their sexual well-being.

- **Hormonal Imbalance**: Stress triggers the activation of the hypothalamic-pituitary-adrenal (HPA) axis, unleashing cortisol and disrupting reproductive hormone equilibrium, impacting ovulation, sperm production, and overall reproductive function. This physiological response extends to neurotransmitters governing mood and sexual function, including serotonin and dopamine. Their imbalances contribute to sexual dysfunction and compromise reproductive health.

Mitigating stress's impact on reproductive health necessitates a holistic approach, merging biblical, medical, and psychological principles. Recognizing individual variations in stress responses is crucial, acknowledging that not everyone faces identical physical health consequences. However, adopting stress management practices, such as mindfulness, prayer, healthy coping mechanisms, and seeking support, significantly enhances overall well-being, reducing the risk of stress-related illnesses. Collaborating with healthcare professionals, counselors, or spiritual advisors allows for tailored guidance and support in addressing the repercussions of stress on mental and physical health. By embracing this multifaceted strategy, individuals can foster resilience and fortify their reproductive health against the detrimental effects of stress.

The Impact of Fasting on Our Physical Health

Fasting holds biblical significance, rooted in profound spiritual traditions. Beyond its spiritual essence, fasting also influences physical well-being. The practice, deeply ingrained in historical and religious contexts, benefits holistic health. Embracing a dual role, fasting resonates with ancient spiritual practices and stands as a testament to its enduring positive effects on the body. Here are ten benefits of fasting as it relates to your physical healing:

1. **Cellular Repair and Regeneration:** Fasting catalyzes autophagy, a process that eliminates damaged cells, paving the way for the regeneration of vibrant, healthy ones. This crucial cellular renewal fosters overall physical health and promotes longevity. By embracing fasting, individuals can actively engage in a natural rejuvenation mechanism, optimizing their well-being on a cellular level. This transformative process enhances the body's resilience. It supports a holistic approach to health, emphasizing the significance of periodic fasting to bolster cellular repair and fortify the foundation of lasting vitality.

2. **Enhanced Insulin Sensitivity:** Scientific studies consistently demonstrate that intermittent fasting improves insulin sensitivity, significantly lowering the risk of type 2 diabetes while fostering balanced blood sugar levels. This dietary approach has proven effective in promoting metabolic health by optimizing the body's response to insulin, a crucial hormone for regulating blood sugar. Embracing intermittent fasting not only supports diabetes prevention but also contributes to overall well-being by maintaining stable glucose levels.

3. **Inflammation Reduction:** Chronic inflammation is a known precursor to numerous diseases. Research indicates that fasting effectively diminishes inflammatory markers, potentially mitigating the risk of inflammatory conditions. Embracing fasting practices may be a proactive approach to bolster overall health by curbing inflammation, consequently promoting well-being.

4. **Enhanced Heart Health:** Fasting can improve heart health by mitigating risk factors, including high blood pressure, cholesterol levels, and triglycerides. Embracing periodic fasting may contribute to a more robust cardiovascular system, fostering overall well-being.

5. **Weight Management:** Embracing intermittent fasting can be a powerful strategy for weight loss, as it regulates hormones and boosts fat metabolism. This approach fosters a healthier body weight and composition by leveraging the body's natural processes. Incorporating intermittent fasting into your routine optimizes hormonal balance, facilitating more effective fat-burning. This not only aids in shedding excess weight but also enhances overall body composition. The method's effectiveness lies in synchronizing with the body's innate rhythms, promoting sustainable and long-term weight management for a healthier lifestyle.

6. **Brain Health and Cognitive Function:** Optimizing Brain Health and Cognitive Function: Fasting is linked to enhanced cognitive performance, encompassing improved memory, heightened focus,

and a shield against neurodegenerative disorders. The practice not only supports mental acuity but also promotes overall brain well-being. Engaging in fasting may fortify neural pathways, fostering resilience against cognitive decline. Embracing this lifestyle choice could be a proactive measure in cultivating a sharp mind and safeguarding against age-related mental challenges.

7. **Boosted Immune System:** Fasting stimulates the generation of fresh white blood cells, fortifying the immune system and amplifying its capacity to combat infections. This proactive approach supports overall immune resilience, potentially reducing susceptibility to illnesses. Embracing fasting as a routine may contribute to a robust immune response, promoting long-term health benefits.

8. **Detoxification:** Fasting is a potent method to eliminate accumulated toxins, effectively cleansing the body. This revitalizing process significantly benefits vital organs like the liver and kidneys. The body expels harmful substances through a strategic fasting approach, promoting overall well-being and optimal organ function.

9. **Longevity Advantages:** Emerging research indicates intermittent fasting may extend lifespan by fostering holistic well-being and diminishing the likelihood of age-related ailments. This dietary approach, characterized by alternating periods of eating and fasting, exhibits potential benefits in enhancing overall health. Individuals may mitigate the risk of age-related diseases by fasting intermittently, contributing to a healthier and more prolonged life.

10. **Improved Gut Health:** Fasting holds the potential to beneficially influence the gut microbiome, fostering equilibrium and a healthful milieu within the digestive system. By abstaining from food for a specified period, individuals may experience improvements in their gut health, creating an environment conducive to overall well-being. This practice has been linked to a more harmonious balance of gut bacteria, contributing to digestive health. Embracing fasting as a mindful health strategy may pave the way for a balanced and

thriving gut, promoting optimal functioning and supporting overall digestive wellness.

Emphasizing the Importance of Healthy Lifestyle Choices, Nutrition, and Exercise

Our daily habits play a pivotal role in shaping the course of our lives and exert a profound influence on our overall well-being. Psychology Today highlights that making intentional decisions to adopt healthy behaviors, such as maintaining consistent sleep patterns, effectively managing stress, and incorporating self-care routines, can significantly impact our physical and mental health.

The significance of fostering a supportive environment that champions healthy choices cannot be overstated. Cultivating relationships with individuals with similar wellness goals, seeking accountability, and nurturing a positive mindset motivate us to make enduring and positive lifestyle changes.

The food we consume holds a key position in determining our physical health. Embracing a well-balanced and nutritious diet equips our bodies with essential nutrients, vitamins, and minerals necessary for optimal functioning. This supports immune function and enhances energy levels, contributing to overall well-being. Intriguingly, our approach to food extends beyond the physical realm and encompasses a spiritual dimension. By practicing mindful eating, expressing gratitude for nourishment, and consciously aligning our food choices with our values, we can cultivate a profound connection with our bodies and the divine, as emphasized in 1 Corinthians 10:31 (NLT): "So, whether you eat or drink, or whatever you do, do it all for the glory of God."
Regular exercise and various activities, such as walking, cycling, dancing, or participating in sports, are pivotal in promoting physical and mental well-being. These activities bring joy and contribute significantly to fostering a healthy and active lifestyle.

A holistic approach to well-being involves making informed choices regarding healthy lifestyle habits, nutrition, and consistent exercise. By prioritizing these facets, we empower our bodies to function optimally, nurture our mental and emotional health, and cultivate an overarching sense of wellness. Making mindful decisions favoring a balanced and active lifestyle can lead to a more fulfilling and enriching life experience.

- **A Prayer for My Physical Healing:** Almighty Father, I come before You with profound humility, earnestly seeking Your divine intervention to restore my physical well-being. I openly acknowledge the pain, illness, or infirmity that currently plagues my body, and I place these burdens at Your feet. In Your boundless mercy and profound healing prowess, I ask You to bestow upon me relief and renewal.

I trust Your infinite wisdom, praying for the strength to endure this trial with unwavering patience and grace. I kindly ask You to guide the hands of those entrusted with my care and to grant them wisdom, particularly if medical intervention such as surgery is deemed necessary. Recognizing You as the ultimate healer, I invoke Your healing light to permeate every part of my being, renewing my physical health.

Please grant me the strength to triumph over this challenging period, and may I emerge from this experience with enriched faith and deep gratitude. May this extraordinary healing serve as a testament to Your glory. I express heartfelt thanks for the healing I am receiving today, firmly believing in the mighty name of Jesus. I offer this prayer with utmost sincerity, Amen.

CHAPTER 7: INTEGRATING THE DIMENSIONS: HOW THE 5 DIMENSIONS SUPPORT EACH OTHER

The five dimensions of healing are intricately intertwined rather than isolated aspects. Our spiritual well-being significantly influences our mental and emotional health, subsequently impacting our relationships and physical state. Recognizing the interconnectedness of these dimensions allows us to adopt a holistic approach to healing, aligning with the wisdom imparted in James 5:16 (NLT): "Confess your sins to each other and pray for each other so that you may be healed. The earnest prayer of a righteous person has great power and produces excellent results."

Healing is not a linear process; instead, it is an ongoing journey. To navigate this journey successfully, it is crucial to simultaneously address and nurture each dimension. This holistic approach synergizes, accelerating our overall healing and transformation. By attending to our spiritual, mental, emotional, relational, and physical well-being concurrently, we open the door to profound growth and restoration. Integrating these dimensions propels us towards a more comprehensive and enduring healing experience.

Our spiritual beliefs and practices profoundly shape our mental well-being. Embracing faith can offer a profound sense of purpose, hope, and tranquility that directly influences our mental state. Incorporating spiritual disciplines such as prayer, meditation, and studying scripture not only supports cognitive health but also nurtures a positive mindset, aligning with the wisdom shared in Romans 12:2(NLT): "Don't copy the behavior and customs of this world, but let God transform you into a new person by changing the way you think. Then, you will learn to know God's will for you, which is good, pleasing, and perfect."

Psychological research further validates the correlation between a solid spiritual foundation and lower levels of anxiety, depression, and stress.

Integrating these spiritual elements can be a transformative journey, contributing significantly to overall mental well-being.

Cultivating our minds with spiritual truths and wisdom is a transformative journey that shapes our thoughts and beliefs. The guidance from the Bible encourages us to continually renew our minds, aligning our thinking with principles rooted in spirituality. Engaging in meditation on scripture, prayer, and a commitment to spiritual growth positively influences our mental well-being.

This renewal process empowers us to break free from negative thought patterns, overcome destructive behaviors, and foster a positive mindset firmly grounded in God's truth. A poignant reminder is found in Philippians 4:8 (NLT), which urges, "And now, dear brothers and sisters, one final thing. Fix your thoughts on what is true, honorable, right, pure, lovely, and admirable. Think about things that are excellent and worthy of praise." Embracing this perspective becomes a guiding principle for nurturing a healthy and resilient mindset by infusing divine wisdom into our daily thoughts and actions.

Numerous studies have demonstrated that incorporating prayer and meditation into one's routine can significantly enhance attention, concentration, and memory. When we deliberately shift our focus toward God and His promises, a cognitive transformation occurs, fostering clarity, heightened focus, and mental resilience. This transformative process is succinctly captured in Isaiah 26:3, emphasizing the profound impact of trust in God: "You will keep in perfect peace all who trust in you, all whose thoughts are fixed on you!"

The nexus between spirituality and mental well-being introduces a profound meaning and purpose. Aligning ourselves with God's purpose and adhering to His principles gives our thoughts and actions a clear sense of direction and significance. Ephesians 2:10 (NLT) reinforces this notion, emphasizing our divine purpose as God's masterpiece, intricately crafted in Christ Jesus to fulfill the good works preordained for us.

An integral aspect of this spiritual alignment is understanding our identity in Christ and as beloved children of God. Embracing our inherent worth, rooted in God's profound love, value, and acceptance bestowed upon us, becomes a catalyst for transforming our mental health. This realization counteracts negative self-talk, dispels feelings of insecurity, and mitigates inadequacy, improving mental well-being. Psalm 139:14 (NIV) encapsulates this transformative truth: "I praise you because I am fearfully and wonderfully made; your works are wonderful; I know that full well."

This chapter delves into practical strategies aimed at seamlessly integrating various dimensions of healing, fostering a comprehensive state of thriving. A pivotal aspect involves the cultivation of consistent daily spiritual practices. Consider initiating each day with prayer, meditation, or scripture reading to harmonize your heart and mind with the truth of God.

Regular worship participation, religious service attendance, or connection with a spiritual community can significantly contribute to your growth. Seek spiritual guidance from mentors, counselors, or pastors who can provide valuable wisdom and support on your transformative journey.

Prioritizing mental well-being is crucial. Practice mindfulness and self-awareness to identify and address negative thoughts or beliefs hindering your healing process. Professional assistance, such as therapy or counseling, may also be beneficial in navigating past traumas, managing stress, and developing healthy coping mechanisms.

Stimulating your mind through activities like reading, learning new skills, or solving puzzles promotes mental agility and growth. Additionally, acknowledge and express your emotions in a healthy, such as through journaling, art, or open conversations with trusted friends or counselors.

Extend self-compassion and self-care to yourself, treating each step of your healing journey with kindness and grace. Learn and implement effective stress-management techniques, including deep breathing exercises, relaxation techniques, or engaging in joyful hobbies.

In your relationships, cultivate open and honest communication by respectfully expressing your needs, boundaries, and emotions. Practice active listening and empathy, seeking to understand others' perspectives and building deeper connections.

Surround yourself with individuals who actively support your healing journey, offering encouragement, accountability, and love. Establish a balanced and nourishing diet by incorporating whole foods, fruits, vegetables, and lean proteins that provide essential nutrients for optimal physical health.

Participate in regular physical activity tailored to your abilities and interests, whether walking, dancing, swimming, or sports. Ensure sufficient rest and sleep, allowing your body time to rejuvenate and heal. Integrating these practices paves the way for holistic thriving and sustained well-being.

Integrating spiritual, mental, emotional, relational, and physical healing is essential for achieving holistic well-being. Our approach to this healing journey involves creating a synergistic blend of practices that work together harmoniously. This transformative path towards wholeness is paved by nurturing our spiritual connection, prioritizing mental well-being, acknowledging and tending to our emotions, fostering healthy relationships, and maintaining the well-being of our physical bodies.

It's essential to recognize that healing is a continuous, lifelong journey. Our practices serve as a sturdy foundation for ongoing personal growth, renewal, and flourishing across all dimensions of life. Embracing this process involves placing trust in the guidance of a higher power, allowing the healing ability of God to permeate and restore abundance to every aspect of our being. Embrace the journey, have faith in the divine guidance, and let the transformative power of healing enrich every facet of your life.

CHAPTER 8: OVERCOMING CHALLENGES; ADDRESSING BARRIERS

Navigating the journey to recovery often requires substantial effort. Along the way, you may encounter challenges that hinder your progress and prevent you from embracing God's healing. This chapter aims to shed light on common obstacles to recovery and offer practical solutions, empowering you to continue moving steadily toward a state of wholeness.

- **Unresolved Issues:** If you find unresolved traumas, wounds, or hurts hindering your recovery, it's crucial to address them actively. Seek professional assistance, such as counseling or therapy, to work through these deeply rooted issues and pave the way for healing.

Consider forgiveness a powerful tool to release grudges and resentment, allowing yourself to break free from the weight of past wrongs. Embracing forgiveness can be transformative and contribute significantly to your overall well-being.

Identify and challenge limiting beliefs and negative self-talk that undermine your self-worth and hinder the healing process. Replace these destructive thoughts with affirmations and biblical truths that reinforce your identity as a cherished child of God.

Surround yourself with supportive communities and positive influences that uplift you, foster personal growth, and cultivate a positive outlook on life. Building connections with those who encourage your well-being can be instrumental in your journey towards healing and resilience.

Stepping beyond the confines of our comfort zones often triggers natural responses like fear and resistance to change. Embracing courage is vital to confronting these apprehensions and confidently navigating uncharted territories, guided by trust in God's direction and provision.

In times of uncertainty and transition, seek guidance and support from reliable friends, mentors, or a support group. Cultivate connections with those who share similar experiences, establishing a network of individuals who can provide encouragement, accountability, and prayer.

Build a community of friends, family, and like-minded individuals committed to supporting you. Utilize their collective strength to foster an environment of love, acceptance, and healing. Engage in faith-based communities, contribute to ministries, and use your abilities, knowledge, and spiritual gifts to create a positive atmosphere.

Explore therapy or support groups tailored to address your specific needs and challenges. Understand that authentic healing is a gradual process that requires time. Embrace grace and patience as you traverse the path of healing.

Set realistic expectations, acknowledge progress amidst difficulties, and celebrate small victories. Surrender control and trust in God's timing and healing plan, allowing faith to guide you through the transformative process.

Overcoming challenges on the journey to recovery requires a combination of bravery, tenacity, and a steadfast faith in the power of God. Recognizing and addressing common obstacles such as unhealed past trauma, self-defeating thoughts, change-related anxiety, a lack of support, and impatience is crucial to breaking free from their hold and continuing on the path to wholeness. It's important to acknowledge that the recovery process is non-linear, and challenges may arise unexpectedly.

Remember that overcoming obstacles is possible, and living the best life that God has planned for you is achievable if you remain committed to seeking God's healing in every aspect of your life. Implement practical solutions and trust His fidelity, relying on His promises. Embrace the freedom that comes with living a healed and complete life. Remember that the journey may not be easy, but with courage, determination, and faith, you can navigate the obstacles and emerge stronger on the other side.

CHAPTER 9: TOOLS AND PRACTICAL APPROACHES TO HEALING

Discover a wealth of invaluable resources and practical strategies meticulously designed to address every facet of your journey toward recovery and wholeness. This comprehensive toolkit encompasses your well-being's spiritual, mental, emotional, relational, and physical dimensions. By seamlessly integrating these resources into your daily life, you have the opportunity to heal and undergo a profound internal transformation. Embark on a holistic approach to your well-being and witness the positive impact on your path to recovery.

- **Mindfulness & Meditation:**

Partake in mindfulness and meditation techniques to cultivate a tranquil mind, alleviate stress, and foster greater self-awareness. The art of mindfulness, a profoundly advantageous skill, involves acknowledging and embracing one's thoughts, emotions, and physical sensations while centering on the current moment. Dedicate a set time each day to engage in mindfulness practices, such as guided meditation or deep breathing exercises. Elevate your presence and attentiveness to the present by seamlessly integrating mindfulness into everyday activities like meals, strolls, or conversations.

- **Writing a Journal:**

Maintain a consistent journaling habit to effectively explore and express your thoughts, emotions, and experiences.

Allow your most intimate reflections to flow freely onto the pages, as uninhibited writing often unveils your most authentic sentiments. Regularly revisiting your diary entries lets you gain insights, identify patterns, and track your journey toward personal growth and recovery.

Engaging in this reflective practice creates a valuable tool for self-discovery and self-awareness. Take the opportunity to delve into your innermost thoughts, providing a cathartic outlet for processing complex emotions. Embrace the power of written expression to capture the nuances of your daily life and foster a deeper understanding of yourself and your evolving narrative.

Incorporating this habit into your routine serves as a means of personal reflection, allowing you to navigate the intricacies of your mind with increased clarity. Over time, writing in your diary becomes a therapeutic exercise, promoting emotional well-being and contributing to your overall sense of resilience.

- **Cultivate Gratitude:**

Cultivating an attitude of gratitude involves intentionally focusing on the positive aspects of your life. Identify at least three things you are thankful for daily, and document them in a gratitude journal. This practice helps shift your mindset towards appreciation.

- **Practice Self-Restraint:**

Demonstrating self-compassion involves treating yourself with love, understanding, and acceptance. Monitor your internal dialogue and replace self-critical thoughts with affirmations that promote self-compassion. Engage in self-care activities that contribute to your overall well-being, recognizing self-compassion as an essential element of your healing journey.

- **Embrace Professional Support**:

Explore the option of seeking guidance from professionals such as coaches, therapists, or counselors who specialize in the specific aspects of your recovery. Expert advice can provide valuable insights, resources, and strategies to facilitate your healing process. Don't hesitate to seek help when needed, and remain open to the guidance and support of qualified professionals.

- **Cultivating Supportive Relationships**:

Surround yourself with individuals who uplift and support your recovery and personal growth journey. Seek out communities or support groups where you can connect with people who have faced similar challenges. Foster meaningful connections built on empathy, trust, and mutual assistance.

- **Engaging in Physical Exercise:**

Incorporate regular physical activities into your routine to enhance your overall well-being and contribute to your physical recovery. Choose activities that bring you joy, such as swimming, walking, running, or even exploring a new dance style. Prioritize your physical health by making exercise a consistent part of your daily life.

In conclusion, integrating these strategies and resources into your life establishes a robust foundation for your recovery process. Each approach addresses different aspects of your well-being, allowing for a comprehensive and holistic recovery. As you explore these techniques and identify the ones that resonate most with you, practice self-compassion and patience. Embrace the journey, have faith in your ability to heal, and trust that these valuable techniques can positively transform all facets of your life when coupled with dedication and support.

DAILY ROUTINES FOR EVERY ASPECT OF RECOVERY

This chapter will explore invaluable activities, skills, and practices designed to support various facets of the recovery process. These resources aim to guide you toward improved physical, relational, mental, emotional, and spiritual well-being. By incorporating these techniques into your daily life, you can foster a holistic approach to healing and witness transformation across every aspect of your overall health.

- **Spiritual Recovery:**

Engaging in a daily prayer routine is essential for your spiritual recovery. Dedicate a specific time each day to connect with God, seeking spiritual guidance and solace. Strengthen your faith by regularly immersing yourself in the passages of the Bible that align with your spiritual principles. Consider incorporating meditation or contemplative prayer into your routine to cultivate a tranquil mind, deepen your spiritual awareness, and fortify your connection to the divine.

- **Mental Recovery:**

Transform your thought patterns by learning to craft positive affirmations that counteract negative ideas and beliefs. Repeatedly reinforce these affirmations to rewire your mind, fostering a more empowered and optimistic mindset. Take proactive steps to recognize and challenge negative thinking patterns, replacing them with practical and constructive alternatives. Incorporate reflective practices, delving into texts that resonate with your recovery journey.

- **Emotional Recovery:**

Expressing pent-up emotions is crucial for emotional recovery. Engage in expressive writing, art therapy, or journaling to release and process your feelings. Cultivate emotional awareness through techniques like body scans and regular emotional check-ins throughout the day. Explore grounding exercises, gradual muscular relaxation, and deep breathing exercises to enhance emotional well-being. These methods empower you to navigate and understand your emotions more consciously.

- **Relationships Recovery:**

Effective communication plays a crucial role in rebuilding relationships, and one key element is active listening. Active listening goes beyond merely hearing words; it involves paying close attention, comprehending the message, responding appropriately, and recalling shared information. To truly engage in active listening, the listener must interact with the speaker, demonstrate empathy, and provide relevant feedback.

Active listeners convey genuine attention and care by maintaining eye contact, nodding in affirmation, and employing vocal cues such as summarizing or seeking clarification. This level of engagement is instrumental in establishing rapport and trust in both personal and professional relationships. The benefits of active listening extend to fostering deeper connections, facilitating effective problem-solving, and improving overall communication.

To enhance your relationships, focus on developing active listening skills. This involves honing the ability to truly understand and communicate more effectively. Building healthier friendships and relationships can also be achieved by mastering constructive conflict resolution techniques, such as using "I statements" and collaborative problem-solving approaches.

Additionally, setting clear and appropriate boundaries within your relationships is crucial for safeguarding your mental health and ensuring mutual respect. Incorporating these practices into your interactions can improve the overall recovery and improvement of your relationships.

- **Physical Recovery:**

Healing can be significantly enhanced through regular physical exercise tailored to your interests and talents. Activities such as yoga, dance, swimming, or walking can contribute to your overall well-being. Additionally, adopting a well-balanced and nutrient-rich diet that includes a variety of whole foods, fruits, vegetables, lean meats, and healthy fats will support your healing journey.

Equally important is incorporating relaxation and sufficient sleep into your routine, as these practices are crucial for allowing your body to repair and rejuvenate.

Fostering healing in every dimension is achievable by integrating these valuable tools and routines into your daily life. It's essential to recognize that the healing process may require self-compassion, perseverance, and patience. Experiment with various tools and techniques to discover what works best for you, positively impacting your overall well-being.

Investigating the Origin of the Five-Dimensional Wounds

The story in the Bible about Adam and Eve's disobedient response to God in the Garden of Eden "messed up" many things for them. Sin negatively impacted their bodies, minds, feelings, relationships, and spirits. Let's take a closer look at what happened, using the Bible as our guide:

In a spiritual context, the transgression of Adam and Eve marked a significant rupture in their once intimate relationship with God. Initially, they enjoyed direct communion with God in the idyllic garden before succumbing to temptation. However, following their consumption of the forbidden fruit, as detailed in Genesis 3:7-8 (NIV), a profound awareness of their nakedness overcame them, leading them to retreat from God's immediate presence. Confronted with their vulnerability, they hastily fashioned makeshift garments from fig leaves to conceal their newfound self-consciousness.

Subsequently, as the man and his spouse wandered through the garden during the tranquil part of the day, they heard the voice of the LORD God. In response to this divine presence, they sought refuge amidst the trees, illustrating the palpable shift in their relationship with the Creator. The advent of sin erected a barrier between God and humanity, prompting the need for spiritual reconciliation.

In essence, the narrative emphasizes the transformative impact of disobedience on the spiritual proximity between humans and the divine, underscoring the necessity for a pathway to reconcile the fractured connection caused by sin.

- **Mentally:** Mentally burdened by shame and remorse, Adam and Eve grappled with the consequences of their transgression and disobedience. The weight of their actions was palpable as they sought to cover themselves with fig leaves, a symbolic gesture reflecting their troubled state of mind (Genesis 3:7). Additionally, their attempt to shift blame further underscores the inner conflict they experienced (Genesis 3:12–13, NIV). In response to God's inquiry, Adam pointed to the woman, saying, "The woman you put here with me gave me some fruit from the tree, and I ate it." The woman, in turn, attributed her actions to the deception of the serpent (Genesis 3:13).

Emotionally, the repercussions of sin manifested in Adam and Eve's overwhelming dread and terror. The paradise they once enjoyed was replaced by a profound loss and sorrow, disrupting their previous state of perfect harmony. This emotional turmoil is evident in their fear of God, anticipating the consequences of their transgression (Genesis 3:10, NIV). Adam's admission, "I heard you in the garden, and I was afraid because I was naked; so, I hid," reveals the depth of their emotional distress in the aftermath of their disobedience.

- **Relationally:** The rupture caused by sin significantly impacted the union of Adam and Eve. In this pre-fall period, they existed in perfect harmony. However, the introduction of guilt and blame created a chasm between them after the transgression. The beauty and unity of their relationship shattered when Adam, in Genesis 3:12 (NIV), pointed to Eve as the cause of his disobedience, stating, "The woman you put here with me—she gave me some fruit from the tree, and I ate it." The corrosive effects of sin on their connection extended to their descendants, manifesting as familiar discord and issues in human relationships.

- **Physically:** Although the biblical account doesn't delve into intricate details, it suggests that Adam and Eve faced physical consequences for their sin. One explicit physical consequence mentioned is the curse on the ground in Genesis 3:17 (NIV). God admonished Adam, saying, "Because you listened to your wife and ate fruit from the tree about which I commanded you, 'You must not eat from it,' 'Cursed is the ground because of you; through painful toil, you will eat food from it all the days of your life." Their transgression led to hardships in labor and agricultural work. Additionally, it is implied that physical mortality and the inevitability of death entered the world due to sin, as elucidated in Romans 5:12 (NIV).

However, amid the consequences of sin, a glimmer of hope emerges in the prophetic promise of Jesus Christ, the future Redeemer. Genesis 3:15 (NIV) states, "And I will put enmity between you and the woman, and between your offspring and hers; he will crush your head, and you will strike his heel." This promise offers hope to those who emphasize repentance, forgiveness, and the pursuit of restoration through faith in God's mercy and grace. The narrative of Adam and Eve's transgression is pivotal in the biblical storyline, serving as a foundational account of the human condition and highlighting the profound need for redemption and reconciliation with God.

CHAPTER 10: LIVING A WHOLENESS-CENTERED LIFE

Let's explore how you can embrace a life centered around wholeness and derive profound benefits from your healing journey now that you possess a deeper understanding of the five dimensions of healing and have incorporated various tools and practices into your daily life.

- **Embrace Mindful Awareness:** Cultivating mindful awareness is pivotal to leading a wholeness-centered life. Hone the skill of being fully present in each moment, attentively observing your feelings, thoughts, and physical sensations. Foster a curious and nonjudgmental mindset as you witness your experiences without immediately labeling them or seeking instant answers. This newfound awareness empowers you to respond to life's challenges with purpose and clarity.

- **Align Your Actions with Your Values:** Living a life rooted in wholeness involves aligning your actions with your core beliefs. Please take a moment to reflect on your fundamental values and assess how each healing aspect aligns with them. Are your actions and decisions in harmony with your values? Identify areas where your activities may be incongruent with your principles and explore ways to make the required adjustments. This process will contribute to a more authentic and fulfilling daily life.

- **Engage in Self-Care:**

- Elevate self-care to the forefront of your priorities, recognizing its indispensable role in leading a life centered around wholeness. Consciously engage in activities that contribute to your mental, emotional, physical, interpersonal, and spiritual well-being.

- Set firm boundaries to protect your precious time and energy. This enables you to unwind, recharge, and indulge in activities that bring joy and fulfillment.

- Understand that prioritizing self-care is not selfish but a fundamental requirement for your overall well-being. By nurturing yourself, you enhance your ability to connect meaningfully with others.

- **Cultivate Meaningful Connections**:

The ability to foster meaningful connections is an essential skill that can significantly impact your life. Surround yourself with individuals who align with your values and support your recovery journey. Actively seek opportunities for meaningful interactions, engaging in deep discussions and sharing experiences. Foster an environment of love, trust, and growth by consistently demonstrating kindness, empathy, and attentive listening in your interactions.

- **Engage in Continuous Learning:**

Embracing a life centered around wholeness requires a commitment to ongoing education and personal development. Acknowledge the benefits of participating in activities that expand your horizons, challenge your assumptions, and introduce new ideas. Whether reading books, attending lectures or workshops, exploring diverse perspectives, or learning from others, lifelong learning will enhance your understanding of the world, others, and yourself.

- **Practice Serving Others:**

An integral aspect of leading a wholeness-centered life is actively seeking ways to contribute to the well-being of those around you. Schedule time for acts of kindness, volunteer for causes you believe in, and extend a helping hand to those in need. Serving others brings fulfillment and a stronger sense of purpose and connection.

- **Maintain Your Commitment to Your Recovery Journey:**

Embracing a life rooted in wholeness demands an unwavering dedication to your ongoing recovery process. Acknowledge that the path to healing involves both highs and lows, and remain resolute in your commitment to the methods, resources, and values that guide you. When faced with obstacles, seek support from your religious community, reliable friends, or experts. Additionally, extend grace and compassion to yourself as you navigate the journey toward wholeness.

Embarking on a life centered around wholeness is a continual process marked by transformative and empowering experiences. Incorporating healing principles into your daily routine can lead to the discovery of authenticity, purpose, and joy. Embrace conscious awareness, align your actions with your regulations, prioritize self-care, cultivate meaningful connections, engage in lifelong learning, assist others, and stay dedicated to your recovery journey. By actively implementing these concepts, you will witness their profound impact on yourself and those in your sphere of influence.

Integrating Wholeness: An Overview of the Main Ideas and Findings

Let's delve into a comprehensive overview of the key concepts and insights derived from the preceding chapters, mainly focusing on the dimensions of healing and the lifestyle practices that pave the way for a life centered around completeness.

- **Spiritual Healing: Re-establishing the Connection with God:** In the initial segment dedicated to healing, we discerned a profound connection between our overall well-being and spiritual completeness. This component highlighted the intricate relationship between our wholeness and spiritual vitality. Exploring the impact of sin on the fracture between humanity and God, we unveiled a pathway to spiritual restoration through the teachings of Jesus. His teachings illuminate a route for healing our spiritual wounds and achieving reconciliation with the divine. Engaging in practices such as prayer, meditation on scripture, and nurturing faith enables us to cultivate a deeper connection with God. This connection, in turn, becomes a source of solace, guidance, and profound meaning in our life journey. This exploration into the realm of spiritual healing underscores the transformative power of these practices, emphasizing their capacity to foster a resilient bond with the divine and illuminate the path toward a more fulfilling existence.

- **Mental Healing: Renewing the Mind for Transformation:** In exploring the impact of ideas and beliefs on mental health, we recognize that the brokenness and lack of security resulting from the sin of Adam and Eve are at the root of mental traumas. However, by renewing our minds with truth, altering negative thinking patterns, and embracing the transformational power of God's Word, we can experience mental healing through Jesus.

- **Emotional Healing: Managing and Handling Our Feelings:** The third aspect of healing focuses on the profound influence of emotions on our overall health. Emotional wounds like shame, fear, and rejection stem from the brokenness caused by sin. Accepting and validating our feelings is crucial to navigate and heal these wounds. Seeking support within our community and finding solace in God's love and grace empower individuals to experience emotional healing through Jesus.

- **Relational Healing: Restoring Connection and Building Good Connections:**

The fourth dimension of healing highlights the value of positive connections in our journey towards wholeness. Relationship injuries, a consequence of Adam and Eve's initial sin, disrupt peaceful coexistence. However, by embracing forgiveness, cultivating compassion and understanding, and establishing genuine, loving connections with others, we can experience relational healing through Jesus. Building and nurturing healthy relationships contribute to restoring links and promoting overall well-being.

- **Physical Healing: Nurturing Our Bodies for Wholeness:** Recognizing the pivotal role of physical health in our overall well-being, we delve into the fifth level of healing. Here, we come to grips with the understanding that bodily wounds, illnesses, and diseases are manifestations impacted by the imperfections of our human existence. This acknowledgment, rooted in recognizing sin's influence, opens the door to the transformative power of physical healing through Jesus.

Making self-care a deliberate priority becomes a foundational aspect of this healing journey. By consciously choosing healthy lifestyles and embracing practices that promote well-being, we actively contribute to restoring our physical selves. Furthermore, seeking medical assistance when necessary is a testament to our commitment to responsibly stewarding the gift of our bodies.

Our pursuit of physical healing becomes a holistic endeavor integrating faith, self-care, and medical support. Through this harmonious approach, we align ourselves with the divine intention for our bodies to thrive. As we engage in this process, we tap into the transformative grace that emanates from our faith in Jesus, fostering a profound sense of wholeness within our physical being.

CONCLUSION
EMBRACING WHOLENESS: A CALL TO ACTION

As I conclude this book, let's reflect on the profound value of this transformative journey and consider the steps you can take to continue progressing toward recovery and holistic health.

- **Embracing a Wholeness-Centered Life:** Proverbs 4:23 wisely advises us to guard our hearts, recognizing them as the wellspring of life. A wholeness-centered lifestyle involves acknowledging the intricate interconnectedness of our spiritual, mental, emotional, relational, and physical facets. Just as Jesus teaches us to love God with our entire being, we must extend that love and care to every part of ourselves.

- **Cultivating Mindful Awareness:** Supported by research in psychology and medicine, mindfulness, rooted in ancient traditions, encourages us to be present and observe our thoughts, feelings, and bodily sensations without judgment. Psalm 46:10 reinforces this, reminding us to "be still and know that I am God." Mindfulness can deepen our connection with God and guide us in making intentional and beneficial choices for our well-being.

- **Committing to Continuous Development and Change:** Pursuing completeness requires self-discipline, endurance, and a willingness to adapt. Drawing inspiration from Philippians 3:13–14, where the apostle Paul urges us to press on, we can engage in healthy lifestyle practices such as prayer, meditation, introspection, counseling, and exercise to promote overall well-being.

Seeking Community and Support: Ecclesiastes 4:9–10 underscores the importance of community on the healing journey, stating that "two are better than one." Look for reliable friends, mentors, and experts to support, accountability, and guidance as you navigate the path to wholeness.

- **Accepting Resilience and Grace:** Recognize that obstacles and setbacks are part of the recovery journey. The Bible is rich with stories of resilience and the sustaining power of God's grace. Embrace failures as opportunities for growth and, during challenging times, extend kindness and compassion to yourself. Romans 8:37 assures us that "we are more than conquerors through Him who loved us." Trust in God's grace, believing that transformation is possible.

As you conclude this book, consider adopting a wholeness-centered lifestyle by drawing inspiration from the Bible, scientific studies, and psychological perspectives. Commit to continuous growth, practice mindful awareness, seek support, and embrace grace and resilience. May your journey lead to profound healing, happiness, comfort, hope, and peace.

The verse from 3 John 1:2, "Dear friend, I pray that all will go well with you and that you may be in good health as it goes well with your soul (NLT)," echoes my prayer for you as you finish reading. Remember that God desires a whole and wonderful life for you (Psalm 139:14 KJV). Utilize the knowledge gained from this book to guide your actions, embracing healing in all dimensions—spiritual, mental, emotional, relational, and physical. Put your trust in the Lord, rely on His promises, and embark on a journey of continuous development, recovery, and health, for with God, all things are possible, including "Total Healing Today!"

- **Closing Prayer:** Heavenly Father, I stand before You with a heart brimming with hope and gratitude as I reach the end of my healing and wholeness journey. Acknowledging You as the ultimate source of healing, I humbly seek Your presence in every aspect of my life. Grant me spiritual healing, strengthening my relationship with You and restoring my faith.

Thank You for providing mental clarity and calmness, enabling me to confront and overcome mental obstacles with fortitude. Replace the emotional scars on my heart with Your peace and joy. Lead me in healing broken relationships, guiding me towards reconciliation, understanding, and forgiveness.

As the Supreme Healer, I trust Your regenerative power to alleviate my physical pain and anguish. Recognizing the boundless nature of Your kindness, grace, and mercies, I release all my worries and problems into Your hands.

I offer this prayer in the name of Your Son, Jesus, my Savior and Lord. I trust that Your healing hands will continue to work miracles in my spirit, soul, and body, as well as in the lives of those who have journeyed through this book. Amen.

If this book has been a blessing to you, please share your thoughts in a review on Amazon.com. Your feedback can help others benefit from the wisdom and insights within these pages. I am sincerely grateful for your support!

Please check out my other book, Saved but Struggling, Well but Wounded: The Benefits of Professional Christian Counseling. **Please scan me!**

You can also check out my other books on Amazon: What Do You Do After You Have Prayed? and, 10 Obstacles to Your Healing. Thank you and blessings today!

ENDNOTES

1. American Academy of Dermatology Association. (n.d.). Stress and Skin. Retrieved from https://www.aad.org/public/everyday-care/skin-care-secrets/stress-and-skin

2. American Psychological Association. (2021). Stress affects the body. Retrieved from https://www.apa.org/topics/stress/body

3. Better Help - "What Is Emotional Intimacy and How to Improve It": https://www.betterhelp.com/advice/intimacy/what-is-emotional-intimacy-and-how-to-improve-it/

4. Christianity Today - "How to Find Healing from Church Hurt": https://www.christianitytoday.com/women/2019/august/finding-healing-from-church-hurt.html

5. Crosswalk - "Seven Keys to Healing from Church Hurt": https://www.crosswalk.com/faith/spiritual-life/seven-keys-to-healing-from-church-hurt.html

6. Feldman, S. R., et al. (2014). The relationship between stress and skin disorders. Clinics in Dermatology.

7. Sound Therapy - "Healing Emotional Wounds: A Guide to Addressing Emotions & Inner Pain": https://www.goodtherapy.org/learn-about-therapy/issues/emotional-wounds

8. Harvard Health Publishing. (2020). The impact of stress on your skin. Retrieved from https://www.health.harvard.edu/newsletter_article/the-impact-of-stress-on-your-skin

9. Healthline - "Fear of Abandonment: Symptoms, Causes, and Treatment": https://www.healthline.com/health/mental-health/fear-of-abandonment

10. Help Guide - "Emotional Abuse: Signs, Symptoms, and Recovery": https://www.helpguide.org/articles/abuse/emotional-abuse.htm

11. https://pubmed.ncbi.nlm.nih.gov/28531770/

12. https://pubmed.ncbi.nlm.nih.gov/30695626/

13. https://www.ncbi.nlm.nih.gov/pmc/articles/PMC4516560/

14. https://www.ncbi.nlm.nih.gov/pmc/articles/PMC5394735/

15. Liao, Y. H., et al. (2009). The impact of psychological stress on acne. Journal of Investigative Dermatology Symposium Proceedings.

16. Life. Church – "The Path to Healing": https://www.life.church/prayer/path-to-healing/

17. Mayo Clinic. (2021). Stress symptoms: Effects on your body and behavior. Retrieved from https://www.mayoclinic.org/healthy-lifestyle/stress-management/in-depth/stress-symptoms/art

18. National Alliance on Mental Illness (NAMI) - borderline personality disorder: https://www.nami.org/About-Mental-Illness/Mental-Health-Conditions/Borderline-Personality-Disorder.

19. National Institute of Mental Health (NIMH) - PTSD: https://www.nimh.nih.gov/health/topics/post-traumatic-stress-disorder-ptsd/index.shtml

20. NIDA - substance use disorders: https://www.drugabuse.gov/drug-topics/substance-use-disorder.

21. NIMH - anxiety disorders: https://www.nimh.nih.gov/health/topics/anxiety-disorders/index.shtml.

22. NIMH - Depression: https://www.nimh.nih.gov/health/topics/depression/index.shtml

23. Psychology Source: DSM-5 (Diagnostic and Statistical Manual of Mental Disorders, 5th Edition).

24. Psychology Today - "Betrayal: It's Not Just About Infidelity": https://www.psychologytoday.com/us/blog/in-flux/201610/betrayal-its-not-just-about-infidelity

25. Psychology Today - "Emotional Wounds": https://www.psychologytoday.com/us/blog/understanding-the-erotic-code/202104/emotional-wounds

Relevant Magazine - "How to Heal from Church Hurt": https://www.relevantmagazine.com/faith/how-to-heal-from-church-hurt/

26. Rieder, E., et al. (2019). Dermatological manifestations of stress in normal and psychiatric populations. Current Psychiatry Reports.

27. Schilling, C., et al. (2019). Stress and reproductive health: A global overview. Journal of Psychosomatic Obstetrics & Gynecology.

28. Sinclair, S., et al. (2011). Stress and female reproductive health: A global perspective. Best Practice & Research Clinical Obstetrics & Gynecology.

29. Sources for mental wounds:

30. Talkspace - "How to Heal Emotional Wounds from the Past": https://www.talkspace.com/blog/how-to-heal-emotional-wounds-from-the-past/

31. The Gottman Institute - "The Four Horsemen: The Antidotes": https://www.gottman.com/blog/the-four-horsemen-the-antidotes/

32. United Nations Population Fund. (2021). Stress and Reproductive Health. Retrieved from https://www.unfpa.org/resources/stress-and-reproductive-health.

33. Unless otherwise indicated, all scriptures are taken from the King James Bible version, copyright 2016.

34. Very well Mind - "The Emotional Wounds That Don't Heal": https://www.verywellmind.com/emotional-wounds-that-dont-heal-4176681.

www.ingramcontent.com/pod-product-compliance
Lightning Source LLC
Chambersburg PA
CBHW060537010526
44119CB00005B/177